Christian Sex Today

I thoroughly enjoyed *Christian Sex Today*! I particularly enjoyed and laughed out loud at the summary of an Old Testament sexual ethic – a real warning against judgmentalism! To find polyamory being explored in a book about Christian sexuality was an eye opener! I found it extremely helpful in terms of how to talk about sex to my daughter when she's older, especially given the unhelpful conservative framework I grew up with.

Rachel Collis
Performer

Jason's unrepentantly honest and unflinching examination of cultural views of sex through time allows the reader to feel released from the constraints of shame that have been imposed by 'the church'. I love how he celebrates the joy of sex and shines a light on the blinded and distorted views that are passed on unexamined to the next generation. Thank you, Jason, for being so brave in exploring such an important aspect of being human. As always I love the intellect, wit, warmth and humour in your writing. Your perspective is a unique contribution to understanding sex as a Christian today.

Jane Grebert,
Science Teacher, Environmental Educator

Sex, evolution, and the Bible… For some Christians, those three words should never be together in the same religious sentence. But Jason John (thank goodness) has put them there - and all with raw and open honesty. I await the prayers and bonfires!

Rex A. E. Hunt
Former chair, Common Dreams Conference of Religious Progressives,
Australia/South Pacific

Few issues are as relevant and in need of level-headed discussion than the one this book eloquently and studiously explores. With flashes of humour and much deep thought, the author takes us, time and again, on a journey from the origins of a belief system to its inappropriate current-day application. This is by no means an 'is there a God' discussion. Rather, it is a 'what is appropriate behaviour for Christians in this modern time and why'. A must read for anyone who seeks to better understand relationships – sexual and otherwise.

Dr Miriam Verbeek
Adjunct Associate Professor,
University of New England Law School

In an era of fundamentalism and fake news, it's refreshing to read a Christian perspective on Creation informed by science and infused with humour.

Tim Cadman,
Research Fellow, Griffith University

LESSONS FROM MOSES,
PAUL, JESUS & DARWIN

CHRISTIAN SEX TODAY

JASON JOHN

COVENTRY
PRESS

Published in Australia by
Coventry Press
33 Scoresby Road
Bayswater Vic. 3153
Australia

ISBN 9780648804475

Copyright © Jason John 2021

All rights reserved. Other than for the purposes and subject to the conditions prescribed under the *Copyright Act*, no part of this publication may be reproduced, stored in a retrieval system, or transmitted in any form or by any means, electronic, mechanical, photocopying, recording or otherwise, without the prior permission of the publisher.

Scripture quotations are from the *New Revised Standard Version Bible*, copyright 1989, Division of Christian Education of the National Council of the Churches of Christ in the United States of America. Used by permission. All rights reserved.

Cataloguing-in-Publication entry is available from the National Library of Australia http://catalogue.nla.gov.au/.

Cover design by Ian James - www.jgd.com.au
Text design by Megan Low (Film Shot Graphics FSG)
Text set in Adobe Caslon Pro

Printed in Australia

Contents

Dedication.. 8
Acknowledgments... 9
Introduction... 11
    The Evolution of Sex 19
    Sex is fun, but that's not why we do it (poem) 19
    Behind the poem................................ 24
    Sexual reproduction evolved..................... 25
    Sex was initially an advantage against pathogens... 26
    Male and female evolved 28
    Sex only very recently became pleasurable........ 32
    There has been a change in the relationship between parenting and sex............................... 32
    Pre-Agricultural sex............................ 40
    Agricultural sex 49

Sex in the Bible.. 51
    Sex in the Old Testament....................... 51
    Sex in the New Testament 62
    Love your neighbour............................ 67

Sex Today... 72
    The premarital window.......................... 72
    Homosexuality.................................. 73
    Masturbation 84
    Changing gender equality, changing marriage advice? 87
    A quick recap 92
    Four paths diverge............................. 94

Sex for *You* Today..................................... 99
    Your environment 99
    Your adaptation................................ 100

A final poem 102
References.. 105

Dedication

Dedicated to the billions of generations of organisms from which I'm descended, especially my mother, who was the first person to read a draft of this book but didn't live to see it published. To Toni, with whom I have continued the reproductive chain unbroken, and with whom sex continues to be fun long after its procreative application ended. To our amazing kids, Finn and Scout, who prove that we must have got something right in our parenting.

And finally, to you, the reader, for reading the dedication instead of skipping straight to the first chapter.

Acknowledgments

This book started as a talk at Yurora, the National Christian Youth Convention in Australia. I'd like to thank the organisers who let me give the talk (twice), the couple of hundred people who came (because it was a youth convention, and mentioned sex), and those who went outside to pray for me. I hope that in this book your prayers were answered.

Miriam Pepper, friend and past colleague, edited several versions of this book, her keen eye and comments were supplemented by Toni Lawson's review of an earlier draft.

Sinead O'Connor, as always, provided most of the soundtrack for the writing of this book, interspersed with songs by Garfunkel and Oates.

Introduction

Christians inherited the Jewish origin stories, recorded in the book of Genesis. These stories shaped our understanding of Jesus, and how to behave as we followed his teachings. Christians today have a vastly expanded origin story, thanks to the insights of cosmologists, geologists, evolutionists, geneticists, ecologists and so on. And thank God for that!

This new origin story, however, has barely penetrated the consciousness of the church. Just over a third of Christians reject evolution completely.[1] If that's you, you might want to skip to 'Sex in the Bible' (Chapter One), but I hope you'll hang in there for this first section. Another third believes, falsely, that evolution and the biblical account of creation can be reconciled. Only a fifth of Christians accept evolution completely, and a substantially smaller proportion have had the time or energy to think deeply about the implications of evolution for their faith.[2] This book will help, at least as far as the sexual and relational aspect of our discipleship.[3] I hope it will also persuade some of the 'reconcilable' third of the need to more deeply embrace the evolution story of our origins, and even encourage the ten percent who are undecided to join us. I hope that if you are an ex or non-Christian, and you live in a culture influenced by Christianity, that you will find the science fascinating, and the faith reflection a stimulus to do your own processing.

---

1   All statistics on evolution are for the Australian Church, in Miriam Pepper, Nicole Hancock, and Ruth Powell, *Church Attenders' Views About Evolution, NCLS Research Fact Sheet 14030*, pp. 8-10.
2   Anecdotally, from many conversations I've had over the years.
3   I've written more broadly on the implications of the evolution story for Christian faith in Jason John, *Worshipping Evolution's God*.

If you were edged out of church, or drifted away, because your sexual practice didn't fit the narrow prescriptiveness of your congregation, perhaps this will provide a way back, or at least nurture your faith and discipleship as part of the church diaspora.

If you sit within the half of the church who think that sex before marriage is sometimes or always permissible[4], this book will provide a solid basis and some good talking points when you engage with the other half, drawing not only on the scientific origin story, but also a close reading of the Old and New Testaments. My greatest hope is that it will encourage you to engage the other half of the church, as so many in the church seem to feel bound by a 'don't ask, don't tell' policy regarding sex before, instead of, or after marriage. It can be a difficult conversation to have, as preserving a 'traditional' approach to marriage and family is ranked as more important to most Australian Christians than tackling poverty.[5]

When I said, 'Thank God' for the new origins story previously, I was not simply being inflammatory for effect. Admittedly, Genesis 2 has much to commend it as a Hebrew Dreaming story which draws strong ecological connections between the *Adam* and the *Adamah*, the Hebrew term for Earth.[6] Genesis 3, however, is a highly problematic explanation of what happened after God released Adam, the servant of the Garden, into Eden:

---

4   Nicole Hancock, Miriam Pepper, and Ruth Powell, *Attitudes to Sex before Marriage, NCLS Research Fact Sheet 14013*.
5   Miriam Pepper et al., *Public Issues and Priorities for Churches, NCLS Research Fact Sheet 13004*.
6   For more on the differences between humanity as servant in Genesis 2, and Lord in Genesis 1, see Normal C. Habel, "Bible Study Session 2 - Humanity Sunday". A longer, more academic consideration is in Theodore Hiebert, "The Human Vocation: Origins and Transformations in Christian Traditions" in *Christianity and Ecology : Seeking the Well-Being of Earth and Humans*, pp. 136ff.

> To the woman [God] said, 'I will greatly increase your pangs in childbearing; in pain you shall bring forth children, yet your desire shall be for your husband, and he shall rule over you'. (Genesis 3:16)

In a single verse, women are punished in perpetuity for Eve's disobedience with the worst pain imaginable, backed up by a divinely implanted biological drive ('Yet your desire shall be for your husband'), and patriarchy is instituted to make sure women don't think for themselves again ('He shall rule over you'). To drive the point home, the man is punished next, and his sin is listening to his wife!

The new Creation stories, revealed in recent centuries, save us from such a vindictive image of God. We now know that birth 'pangs' are not divine punishment, but are the inevitable, painful result of bipedal creatures with thickened pelvises giving birth to intelligent babies with correspondingly big heads.[7]

As the sciences uncover the story of our origins, the divinely entrenched patriarchal dynamic in Genesis 3 gives way to an appreciation of just how much human relationships are shaped by their environment, as is the case for all creatures. Sexual relationships evolve and adapt to the environment in which creatures live. This is as true for snails as it is for humans. So, if humans live in different environments, we would expect that their sexual relationships will differ.

The environment in which you and I live is remarkably different from that of our subsistence, hunter-gatherer ancestors. In most of the world, it is notably different from that of the Jews who wrote the Torah, which is itself different to the world of the

---

7   Jason John, "Biocentric Theology: Christianity Celebrating Humans as an Ephemeral Part of Life, Not the Centre of It" (Flinders University, 2005), pp. 150ff.

first Christians. Our environment is even different from that of our parents and, when we think about it, even from others in our own generation.

Homo sapiens spent approximately 190 thousand years primarily as hunter gatherers. Only in the last 10 thousand years or so has a predominantly agricultural approach to life spread to most parts of the world. Industrialisation is an even more recent innovation. Therefore, the vast majority of your human ancestors were at least semi-nomadic and relied heavily on hunting and gathering. These many ancestors lived in very small communities, where there was far more equality, and probably a lot more sharing and collaboration including, at least sometimes, sharing of sexual activity.

When they wrote the Torah, the Jewish authors incorporated some stories from their nomadic past, but were a settled agricultural people who had developed a thoroughly patriarchal culture. They experienced constant skirmishes with their neighbours and were eventually overthrown. Their leaders were taken into captivity in Babylon and, surrounded by the most powerful and technologically advanced culture in their region, they compiled their stories into the scriptures we know today. They longed for political restoration, a return to their homeland to rebuild the Kingdom on Earth (documented in Ezra). Marriage and family – pure Jewish family – was the key to rebuilding the race, and it was important to know what belonged to whom as they began the task of restoring the Kingdom of Israel.

After the Temple was destroyed by the Romans, early Christian hopes moved from a physical kingdom being rebuilt, to a Godly Kingdom descending apocalyptically from the heavens (Revelation 21). The end was nigh. Jesus was about to return. Marriage and family were therefore distractions to be avoided. Property was an encumbrance to be discarded.

These days, few Christians seriously believe that the end is nigh, especially in the West, as seen by our tendency to hold on to our property. We live in a different world from the first Christians, with a different mindset. For example, most Christians see marriage as an ideal, rather than sharing Paul's view that it was a concession to those who 'burn with passion' (1 Corinthians 7:9) and cannot handle a life of single-minded devotion to God (1 Corinthians 7:25-35).

We even live in a different world from our parents. My parents grew up when Catholics and Protestants wouldn't marry each other, and women had to resign from employment upon marriage. Patriarchy, homophobia, and racism were in full swing. Australia was mostly white, partly because of Government policy, and universities were full of Australian students, who received a free education. When they finally got a family phone it was attached to the wall. The world was analogue.

Our environment is also different from most of our peers, even if we live in the same city. We have diverse levels of wealth, education, family structures and origins, different disabilities, and our gender is different from half of our peers at least. Unless you are a Generation X, over educated, divorced and remarried white Australian male, your environment is different from mine, so how you choose to act as a romantic and sexual person is bound to be different too. Not because one of us is more moral or faithful, but because we are applying the fundamentals of our faith in different environments.

So, each of us needs to discern what kinds of relationships and sexual activity are best suited to the environment we live in, as we try to follow the way of Jesus in the twenty-first century. What does it mean to love God, neighbour, and self, and to do for others as we would have done for us, in terms of our sexuality and relationships, in the light of what the new Creation stories tell us about where we came from and who we are?

This book hopes to help us answer that question by working through the evolution of sex and sexual relationships. We start at the dawn of life, then move rapidly to the first *Homo sapiens*, who walked the earth for 200 thousand years or so, having inherited their sexuality and sexual behaviour from their primate ancestors, adapting it to the new 'environment,' of having larger brains and more complex social capabilities. We see that their relationships reflect their environment, particularly their relative lack of wealth, and their need to work together to survive.

We then look at the Old Testament approaches to relationships, as an example of our early agricultural existence, in a time when men dominated this new world of possessions and property. Examining the New Testament approaches to sexual relationships highlights that there is no one biblical approach to marriage or sex. Unlike the authors of the Hebrew Scriptures, the early Christians find themselves in a new Greco-Roman world, as an occupied minority waiting for the imminent return of the Messiah.

Then we move to twenty-first century Christianity. How have things changed since Jesus' day? We look at the new gap between the onset of puberty and marriage, and the increasing equality, in many parts of the world, between women and men, including women's increasing financial independence. We then take a quick look at three modern flashpoints: homosexuality, masturbation and adultery. What has the church taught about them, and what alternative understandings do the scientific creation stories have to offer?

Christians, in their obsession with homosexuality, rarely pay any attention to the evolutionary creation story, instead focusing on a few passages in the Bible, and especially Paul's letters. But we need to get our heads around the very different worldviews of Paul and his contemporaries, including their total ignorance of homosexual orientation, and perhaps their patriarchal revulsion that a man could allow himself to be used like a woman. We also need to remember all the other "abominations" condemned alongside male on male sex in the Old Testament, which many of us practise, for example the charging of interest on loans.

The damage done by the church in its teaching about homosexuality has a close rival in its teaching about masturbation, or "self-abuse". By deliberate infliction of harm to stop it, and preventing humans from enjoying its many medically demonstrated health benefits, the church has accumulated a great moral debt. Masturbation is healthy not only for the practitioner, but possibly also for their partner.

Adultery, or infidelity, rounds out the three hot topics. How do we use our new knowledge of our evolutionary past to understand it? Do we open the door to non-judgmental acceptance of the inevitability of extra-marital sex? Do we opt for serial monogamy not just before marriage, but instead of it? Or do we use these insights to help us maintain passionate life-long monogamy?

How do the insights of the new evolutionary Creation story inform our discipleship in our current environments? What other questions can we ask ourselves to get to the heart of faith-full sexual relationships in the twenty-first century, in the light of the new stories about our Creation which the sciences are uncovering? We will see that what we call traditional marriage in the West isn't particularly traditional, isn't divinely mandated from the beginning of Creation, and so is no longer unquestionably the only sphere within which faithful disciples can morally enjoy sexual relationships. Nor is there an automatic guarantee that a marriage relationship is a moral one, as the statistics on domestic abuse make disturbingly clear.

When I gave the talk that led to this book, I explained how I came to some of my conclusions, and the science on which they were based, in a poem. If you hate poetry, and indeed if you love good poetry, skip ahead. Otherwise, for your information and hopefully amusement, read on,

The Evolution of Sex

Sex is fun, but that's not why we do it (poem)

Many years ago, my church wrote 'Uniting Faith and Sex'
We got stuck on gays and lesbians but there was much more in
    the text
It spoke of right relationships, in marriage and outside
It spoke of sex as self-transcending, spiritual, divine.

But it was so very serious, in a very churchy way
That by the end I felt compelled to write to them and say –
Sex is fun!
That's why we do it!
Why we do it when you get down to it –
When you get down to it,
When all is said and done
We have sex because sex is fun!

But then I did more reading:
(for a taxpayer funded PhD)
And I came to the conclusion that I was wrong, you see…
But before I tell you more about sexual reality
Let me say a little more about the man called me.

People call me Jason, I've honours in zoology
I'm also a minister, who has passed theology.
I studied up on evolution to complete a PhD.
And I've been a bloke for years, about forty-three.

So, I can say, after years of study
And more contemplation
And a little bit of practice and my share of consternation…

Sex is fun
but that's not why we do it,
It's only fairly recently that evolution grew it!

Of course, most creatures of Earth don't even do it at all
They just split in half and then off they crawl
Then homosexuality was the first revolution,
There was only one sex for most of evolution.

Now we have sexes, but not just two –
Some species have dozens. Yes, it's true!
Then we have all those whose gender bends
They switch back and forth – it never ends!
Fish girls become boys become women become men
A cycle repeating again and again.

Even when our sex stays fixed
Things can still get a little mixed:
XO, XX, XXX, XXXX, XXXXX
(that's just the female sex!)
Also XY, XXY, XXXY, XXXXY, XYY
Yes, all kinds exist on the male side.

And if you think that's a little absurd –
The whole thing is reversed in those feathery birds!

I am an XY, a boy bird's a ZZ
And there may be more we don't know about yet!

Sea sponges can have sex, or do it alone,
Yes, on a whim they can mate, or clone.

Of course, when they have sex there is no penetration
They just squirt it all out and hope for fertilisation.
Those sponges have orgies to an unheard-of degree,

Think about that when you swim in the sea!

Creatures that do penetrate usually have no fun
Just to survive is the main rule of thumb.
Male spiders get eaten unless they are clever,
Lots do it once, most bees do it never.

Birds orgasm in the blink of an eye,
Antechinus do it then crawl off to die.
But bonobos do it with whomever they can,
Then they do it again and again!

Sex seems to be fun for so many primates
Especially bonobos and us hairless apes.

But sex is dangerous, you get dead a lot.
So why didn't life just say, 'I'd rather not'.
Sex in all its forms has evolved
To help us fight off the common cold!

Well, really to fight off the deadlier types
Of viruses, bacteria and even parasites.

We shuffle the deck when we combine our gametes
It's infections by germs which sex evolved to defeat!

Sure, we love sex now, we think it's great!
But it started to let us recombinate
If there were no germs there would be no sexuality –
A whole lot of fun just to avoid a great calamity!
All this fuss, all this ingenuity
Just to help each species hang around in perpetuity
Mating involves danger, rituals and mess
Yet humans keep on mating – though we're breeding less.

Now, whilst drawing morals straight from evolution
Is really pretty dumb
So is quoting Genesis
Like some God given rule of thumb.
Like... some say God made Adam and Eve, not Adam and Steve,
Now we know that's just rubbish
First all sex was same sex and didn't life flourish!
While I can't vouch for bloke to bloke, about it many rave,
Or when there's only women – for some friends that's the fave.

Often at a wedding you will hear that God gave marriage
I tend to think it's just a bit of Genesis inspired baggage.
Evolution tells us that it certainly took a while.
And it's not like Western monogamy is the only human style.

Sure, marriage is great for a stable society.
The very thing Jesus threatened – he died a man of notoriety.

Yet my wife and I subscribe to it, using contraception
(well most of the time, there's been two conceptions)
A lovely little kid, and another just arrived.
The planet's overcrowded yet we're still glad they survived.

Other friends have no kids, though they have often tried.
It doesn't help when people say it's for God to decide!
Babies come when a sperm makes it to an egg
Not when God decides it – we do not have to beg.

Now, sex to get our kids was a highlight bar none,
But we're not having any others, and sex is still fun.
It was even more fun after I got the snip
Lucky I'm not Catholic but a Protestint!

Another thing that could be good, if you want to try and see
Is some time, short or long, of celibacy.
Though it's caused its share of problems, when the church enforced it
Thinking that the end was nigh, Jesus and Paul endorsed it.

I agree that sex is great –
For a married woman and a man.
The problem is that some then say
That nobody else can.

The Evolution of Sex

But any ethic which ignores the fact that we've evolved
Is an ethic that will leave many problems still unsolved.
I cannot give you all the answers in a silly little poem
Or if I did it would not rhyme
and I can't stand that.

Love yourself love your neighbour
Do for them as you'd have done
Jesus' simple little rules
make sex both fair and fun

Should you go and have sex?
Well I can't pretend to know...
If you haven't started yet, then be careful as you go
Sex should be a lot of fun
But it isn't always so!

Sex is spiritual, mystical, emotional, relational
Luminous, numinous, even educational
The Bible had a point when it says it makes us one.
Even if it started to avoid a pathogen!

Behind the poem

It is essential to understand our evolutionary origins if we are going to make sense of, and live well with, our sexuality. Of course, we can't argue directly from evolution to morality and ethics. Evolution doesn't say all there is to say about marriage and sex, but if what we try to say isn't at least consistent with what we know from the evolutionary sciences, it's likely to be wrong. At best it will be built on a shaky foundation.

I want to expand on some of the points in the poem, about the evolution of sex itself, before we focus in on human sexuality. Our new Creation stories tell us that:

Sexual reproduction evolved.

Sex was initially an advantage against pathogens.[8]

Male and female[9] individuals evolved from hermaphrodites,[10] which evolved from unisexual ancestors.

Sex only very recently became pleasurable.

Let's look at each point in more detail.

Sexual reproduction evolved

When life evolved nearly four billion years ago, all organisms reproduced asexually, that is without sex. Single-celled organisms simply split in half and reformed two identical copies repeatedly. Occasional mutations provided the variation for natural selection to act upon. Eventually a kind of proto sex evolved, where single-celled organisms injected some of their genetic material into other cells, and this was incorporated into the receiving cell's genome.[11] This process, called conjugation, continues today amongst bacteria,

---

8   Pathogen is the umbrella term for infectious microorganisms like viruses, bacteria and fungi.
9   Male defined as having small, mobile gametes (sex cells) called sperm, and female as having larger, usually non-mobile gametes, or eggs.
10 Hermaphrodites are organisms which are both male and female.
11 Various, "Bacterial Conjugation" (see **References**)

and allows them to share abilities like resistance to antibiotics, or the ability to digest a different food source.[12]

After two billion years of sex-free reproduction, single-celled eukaryotes[13] evolved. With eukaryotes came sex, but not as we know it. At first, all reproduction was homosexual, or same-sex.[14] Then hermaphroditism followed as an intermediate stage[15], before most of our eukaryotic ancestors settled on heterosexuality.[16] Before we get into to that, it's important to ask why we have sex at all.

Sex was initially an advantage against pathogens

Why have sex when it's quicker, easier and safer to just split in half? There must be some good reason because nearly all eukaryotes reproduce sexually, though a few have returned to their asexual ways. Sex is everywhere, which puzzled scientists for over a century.[17] Sexual reproduction is more difficult, slower, and more dangerous. It means also that each parent only passes on half of

---

12   Ibid.
13   These single celled eukaryotes are the ancestors of all plants and animals.
14   It was indeed single-celled. The first sexual reproduction was in our single-celled eukaryotic ancestor (Various, "Evolution of Sexual Reproduction". See **References**). The first multicellular organisms were homosexual or unisexual too, as sponges are today, for example.
15   University of Pittsburgh, "Two from One: Evolution of Genders from Hermaphroditic Ancestors Mapped Out".
16   Plants, however, retain a dazzling array of approaches to sex, mostly hermaphroditic. Heterosexuality is far from the only choice for animals. See the figures on pages xviii and following of Leo Beukeboom and Nicolas Perrin, *The Evolution of Sex Determination*.
17   Ernst Mayr, *What Evolution Is*, p. 115.

their genes to their offspring. By contrast, asexual organisms can reproduce at will, with negligible risk, and pass on all their genes. Why, then, go to all the trouble? Why has natural selection not eliminated such a costly process? Indeed, not all species persisted with sex: some reverted to asexual reproduction and others, like sea sponges, stick insects, and at least one species of snake[18] kept both modes: sometimes they clone, sometimes they reproduce sexually.

The answer almost surely lies in the major difference between sexual and asexual reproduction. In the latter, the only source of genetic variation comes from mutations, which are rare, and at least as likely to be harmful as helpful. In sexual reproduction, the DNA of two individuals is 'shuffled', leading to significant variation in every generation of offspring. This variability means that, in the event of a major change in the environment, it is more likely that at least some individuals will have the qualities necessary to cope, or even thrive. Sex, in other words, exists to promote diversity, to help species survive a constantly changing environment. One very significant change in the environment is caused by pathogens,[19] which constantly mutate into new strains. Sex is largely a selective response to disease and parasitism.[20] Early eukaryotes were simple creatures with short life-cycles, but not as short as that of viruses and bacteria. Sexual reproduction sped up the generation of genetic diversity, allowing our ancestors to stay one step ahead of disease. Eventually, as eukaryotes became larger and even slower breeding, we evolved immune systems that could adapt within an individual's lifetime to the ever-changing viruses and bacteria afflicting us.

---

18   Various, "ZW Sex-Determination System" (see **References**).
19   The next few paragraphs are based on Zimmer's extensive treatment of sex, see Carl Zimmer, *Evolution: The Triumph of an Idea*, pp. 229ff.
20   Mayr, *What Evolution Is*, p. 116. For an extended treatment see Zimmer, *Evolution: The Triumph of an Idea*, p. 229ff.

Male and female evolved

All sex was initially homosexual, in that there was only one sex.[21] Individuals produced gametes with half of the required DNA and released them into the environment. When their gamete combined with the gamete of another individual, a new creature was formed. This undercuts the assumption of many Christians, based on Genesis 1, that God created the world heterosexual, and so by implication everything else is an unnatural deviance from God's plan.

Initially, individuals released their gametes into the water in much the same way as sponges reproduce today. This is pretty hit and miss, so sponges release billions of sex cells in the hope they will bump into somebody else's sex cells. Most gametes are wasted so, over hundreds of millions of years, natural selection favoured a system which included both mobile gametes (the precursor of sperm) and sedentary ones (eggs). Originally, each organism had both kinds of gametes; the world was hermaphroditic, as it remains for most flowering plants.

Some animals also refused to commit to one gender or the other and remained hermaphroditic, as in the case of snails. Each snail has male and female sex organs and sex consists of the struggle of each snail to impregnate the other, since it's easier to make new sperm than grow and hatch eggs. They literally attempt to stab each other with their penises and ejaculate into each other. Noah could have grabbed any two snails for his ark and it would have been fine. The flood story in Genesis 6 assumes that all creatures are male or female. Its authors knew nothing of asexuality, monosexuality, hermaphroditism, temperature dependent sex, changing sex, or

---

21 We could also call it unisexual, or monosexual. But those terms have been defined in the literature to refer to other aspects of reproduction.

even multi-sex species. Slime moulds, for example, have *hundreds* of different sexes.[22]

For those species that did evolve into sperm-carrying males and egg-carrying females, the sex of each individual was usually not determined by its genes, but environmental factors, especially the temperature of its egg. This is still the case for most reptiles.[23] Sex could even change throughout life, as it does in several surviving species of fish.[24]

We have barely scratched the surface here. Olivia Judson explores the mind-bending diversity of ways in which animals' sex lives have adapted to their environments. Along the way she demonstrates the near ubiquity of female promiscuity[25] and the vanishingly small number of species that are truly monogamous.[26] If you read her book, you will see that when we get to the section on masturbation, we are in good company with a strange array of other species which also indulge.[27] Our ancestral history is full of gender-fluid species[28], especially fish, many of which change genders throughout their lives. Bisexuality is also widely

---

22 Judson, *Dr Tatiana's Sex Advice to All Creation (Kindle Version)*, p. 196ff. There are far more mechanisms for determining the sex of individuals in various species than I've mentioned here, summarised in Various, "Sex-Determination System" (See **References**.)
23 Bruce Lahn and David Page, 'The Evolution of the Sex Chromosomes: Step by Step'.
24 Judson, *Dr Tatiana's Sex Advice to All Creation (Kindle Version)*, p. 187.
25 Ibid. p. 9.
26 Ibid., p. 152.
27 Ibid., p. 87.
28 Ibid., pp. 196ff.

practised.[29] Stop to think for a moment about how different that is from the biblical picture of two distinct, universal and immutable sexes. How different might our attitude be to homosexuality and transgenderism if we grew up with the actual history of sex and gender, not a biblical model that is completely ignorant of all this history and diversity?

How differently might we have conceived of 'male' and 'female?' Amongst mammals, males might often be the more physically powerful sex, but amongst our kindred species they are often puny[30], just like our little shrivelled sex chromosome.[31]

In most mammals, the female has two similar sex chromosomes (XX), while males have one X and one stunted chromosome called Y. Contrary to Genesis 2, males were not created first, and contrary to Aristotle and Aquinas, women are not misbegotten or malformed men.[32] The Y chromosome is the product of a mutation, which caused one chromosome of a regular pair to trigger maleness, overriding environmental sex determination. This chromosome subsequently withered[33], into the puny little Y chromosome we see today. A Y chromosome is a

---

29   Ibid., p. 142. Although Judson talks about homosexuality, it is clear from her examples that the animals involved are not exclusively homosexual.

30   Ibid., pp. 198ff. Male puniness often varies markedly within a species (even more so than in humans), with males adopting one of two strategies – the hunk, or the runt (ibid., pp. 76-90.) Here again, the males' approach to sexual "relationships" is affected by their environment, i.e. their own size.

31   Chromosomes are pieces of DNA, which contain all our genetic code. The numbers vary widely. Humans have 46, chimpanzees have 48, but goldfish have 100!

32   Thomas Aquinas, *Summa Theologica*.

33   Lahn and Page, 'The Evolution of the Sex Chromosomes: Step by Step'.

misbegotten X. Even this simple dual-sex system we all think of as 'normal' has some surprises. In birds and some fish, the genetics are completely reversed relative to mammals. Male birds are designated ZZ because their sex chromosomes are the same, and females are ZW. Even within mammals there is diversity. XY is the dominant system, but as if they were not weird enough already, platypus males are not XY, but XYXYXYXYXY![34]

The take home message from the evolution of this dizzying diversity is that the creation of male and female in the new Creation story coming from the sciences is far from universal and is more complicated than appreciated by the writers of Genesis, who assumed that all species have always had just two sexes.

Creation Stories Compared

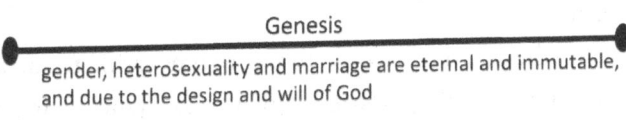

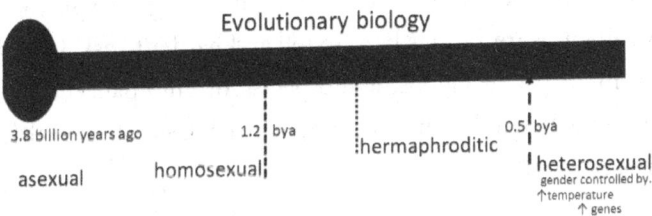

FIGURE 1- Creation Stories Compared[35]

---

34 Wesley C. Warren et al., "Genome Analysis of the Platypus Reveals Unique Signatures of Evolution."
35 Slide from Jason John, *Sex & Relationships: From the Origins of Life to the Life of the Twenty-First Century Church.*

Genesis 1 is a Creation story in which everything is *fixed* and *planned* ('and God said… and there was…'). But the evolution of life, including sex, reproductive strategies, parenting/partnering strategies, and community structure is *fluid and adaptive,* and *driven by environment and context.*

Sex only very recently became pleasurable

As recounted in the opening poem, for most of life's story, sex hasn't been much fun. Indeed, it has often been dangerous. Although courtship rituals may be long and elaborate, once the sex act begins it is usually over as quickly as possible. Nobody wants to be caught in the act by a predator. Passing on genes is more important than pleasure, or even survival.

Eventually sex did become fun, for some primates at least, to the extent that they started having sex quite apart from reproduction, and even alone. My friend's dog also seemed to enjoy self-pleasure, but it's hard to tell and harder to ask. One does not want to pry. Bonobos, a subspecies of chimpanzee, indulge often. Long, languid sexual encounters reach their climax with our species, especially in recent times.

There has been a change in the relationship between parenting and sex

In the evolutionary story of life, we started out with no parents at all. Our ancestors just cloned themselves and each clone floated off on its merry way. With the arrival of sex, we had parents, but there was no parenting. Gametes were simply squirted out into the ocean. If they met, a baby formed, which had to look after itself. Even in more complex animals, like many reptiles and some birds, babies have no contact with their parents. The eggs are hidden in a safe, warm place, and that's it. Sometimes babies end up being food for their parents, or their siblings.

Eventually, in a few species, a dazzling array of parenting styles evolved. Think of the range from pocket frogs to crocodiles, to chickens, rabbits, monkeys and us. All mammals, who by definition feed their babies via their mammary glands, have a close bond with their mother, or a surrogate mother, for at least a brief time. Until very recently, if a strong bond was not formed between a mother and offspring, the offspring would soon die. Any genetic disposition to strong bonding, by both infant and mother, was therefore very strongly selected for by evolution. Still, the diversity of parenting styles amongst mammals is staggering. As humans spread around the globe, developing new cultures to help us survive in each new environment, there were massive changes in the relationship between sex and parenting *within* our species, because our brains let us modify our behaviour so markedly. One commonality is that, relative to other mammals, our babies need intensive parenting for a *long* time, because we need to be born relatively prematurely, before our brains get too big to fit through the birth canal.[36] I've said more about the evolution of our brains and some of the implications for our relationships and faith in *Worshipping Evolution's God*.[37]

All the early species of *Homo*, stretching back two million years, were nomadic groups or tribes with few possessions. *Homo sapiens*, our species, continued to live that way, or very close to it, for the first 190 thousand years or so of our existence, or 95-99.5 per cent of our history. All this time, we were nomadic groups with

---

[36] Full human gestation, if head size was not an issue, would be about 21-26 months according to Richard Southwood, *The Story of Life*, p. 226. See also Mayr, *What Evolution Is*, p. 274.
[37] John, *Worshipping Evolution's God*.

little or no property to worry about. It is difficult to know what our sexual relationships were like back then. Comparisons to modern hunter gatherers are complicated because even where they have had little direct contact with agriculturalists and industrialists, they seem to be under considerable resource stress, driven by shrinking territories. They therefore live in environments different from our ancestors, who numbered in the thousands to millions, and who were subject to millennia-long fluctuations between plenty and scarcity.

As agriculture finally developed, humans entered a grey area between true nomads and permanently settled agriculturalists. In this environment, sexual relationships, though far from monogamous, were sometimes strictly controlled. For example, Aboriginal communities in Australia had very complex marriage laws, including polygamy.[38] Only recently has the veil of European agricultural prejudice been lifted enough to appreciate the many ways in which Aboriginal people manipulated the landscape, and created towns, fields, irrigation schemes and the like, as described in books like *Dark Emu* and *The Biggest Estate on Earth*.[39] Most Aboriginal communities continued to move with the seasons, hunting and gathering, and returning to their settlements annually.

For centuries, agriculture was seen to be such an obvious good that cultures which didn't seem to have embraced it could be replaced without too much guilt on the part of various conquerors

---

38 In 2018, as the Uniting Church in Australia debated whether to allow its ministers to marry same-sex couples, the President formally apologised to Aboriginal people for the church's insistence that Aboriginal candidates have only one wife, and the harm that had caused the other wives who were abandoned. (Stuart McMillan, *Retiring Address to the 15th Assembly of the Uniting Church in Australia*.)

39 Bruce Pascoe, *Dark Emu Black Seeds: Agriculture or Accident*; Bill Gammage, *The Biggest Estate on Earth: How Aborigines Made Australia*.

from more "advanced" societies. But a few scholars question the widespread assumption that the shift from nomadic to agricultural life represented a great leap forward for humanity, an unambiguous improvement. Jared Diamond argues that in embracing agriculture, '… we made the worst mistake in human history. Forced to choose between limiting population or trying to increase food production, we chose the latter and ended up with starvation, warfare, and tyranny'.[40] If Diamond is right, perhaps agriculture itself was the apple in Eden, and life-long monogamous marriage is the result of 'the worst mistake in human history'.

In any case, with settled agriculture it was possible to pass property down through generations. With the idea of inheritance, certainty about biological descendants became important, or at least more important. Since many sexually transmitted diseases appeared when humans started to domesticate animals,[41] and contraception was unreliable, sex and pregnancy were closely related, and virginity (for women) was prized as a guard against both cuckolding and possibly disease. We see this codified in the Hebrew Scriptures.

Only extremely recently, after the development of better contraceptives, more effective condoms, medical treatments for STDs, and safe abortion for those open to it have we started to create a world where sex can be had purely for fun.[42] As we will see later, this is even more the case for those who have been able to get away from the male-centred understanding of 'proper sex' as being intercourse, especially when women are financially independent.

---

40 Jared M. Diamond, "The Worst Mistake in the History of the Human Race"
41 Melissa Lafsky, "How Often Do Animals Get STDs?"
42 Even when women in many parts of the world get pregnant, it is increasingly feasible to raise the baby without the help of a partner.

The creation story, which Christians have worked with for about 2,000 years, implies that the fundamental nature of life, relationships and sex is *fixed*. It is static by divine design. But the creation story science reveals is that all of life, including sexual dimorphism, reproductive strategies, parenting strategies, and forms of relationships, are fluid and adaptive. Life, and sex, is driven and shaped by the environment or context in which various species live. We will see that this is even true in the Old and New Testaments, and ask what it means for us as twenty-first century Christians. Many of today's Christians live in a decreasingly sexist world, which we no longer believe is about to end, and where sex is not always about having babies, but can be about fun and strengthening bonds between people.

Who can have that fun? In church, the widespread claim is that sexual pleasure is legitimate only in the context of lifelong monogamy. Even a more progressive church like the Uniting Church in Australia, which ordains women, has gay and lesbian ministers, and allows its ministers to officiate at gay marriages, still assumes in its proposed new marriage liturgy that marriage is a prerequisite for a couple to be sexually active.[43] In support of this, Christians glossed over most of the Old Testament, and the ambivalence of Jesus and Paul to marriage, and focused on the later New Testament writings that deal with the church's place in a world which, to their surprise, hadn't ended after all. I don't think I was the only one, as a new Christian, who also drew on the many comforting examples in the natural world of monogamous creatures, who seemed to lend weight to the idea that monogamy, if not universal, was at least common, and natural, and God ordained, even if our divorce courts show that many humans find it a challenge.

---

43 "The companionship and comfort of marriage enables the full expression of physical love." (Uniting Church in Australia, *Uniting Church in Australia Additional Marriage Liturgy*.)

Unfortunately for those reassured by the many monogamous species around us, closer investigation by ecologists reduced monogamy to a tiny island in a sea of polygamy. Or as Zimmer puts it, "Promiscuity is rampant in the animal world, even in species that generations of scientists had been convinced were utterly faithful."[44] For example, amongst birds, though 90 per cent of species are socially monogamous – that is they live with one partner – up to 55 per cent of chicks are the product of clandestine liaisons, depending on the species.

In humans, extra-marital pregnancies vary according to changes in the environment. Over one third of the children born in Britain between 1939 and 1945 (during WWII) were illegitimate.[45] In societies not under such duress, estimates range from 0.8 percent in Switzerland to 30 percent in the southern UK, with an average of 3.7 percent.[46] A more recent study suggests a figure closer to 1-2 per cent,[47] but we must remember that *all these studies* give the rates for *pregnancies* which actually made it to term. The rates of extra-marital sex would have been much higher again. Edward Fernandes lists studies reporting 20-75 percent.[48]

---

44 Zimmer, *Evolution: The Triumph of an Idea*, p. 240.
45 An archaic word referring to a person's "legitimate" claims on their father's property. The statistics are from John Costello, *Love Sex and War: Changing Values, 1939-45*, pp. 276-7. Potts and Short mention a study in one town, Romford, where the figure was only 25 percent (Malcolm Potts and Roger Short, *Ever since Adam and Eve: The Evolution of Human Sexuality*, p. 85.)
46 Mark A. Bellis et al., "Measuring Paternal Discrepancy and Its Public Health Consequences".
47 Maarten Larmuseau et al., "Cuckolded Fathers Rare in Human Populations".
48 Edward M. Fernandes, "The Swinging Paradigm: An Evaluation of the Marital and Sexual Satisfaction of Swingers.", pp. 8, 10.

Extra marital sex has a very deep, ancestral history, according to Malcolm Potts and Roger Short.[49] Human sexual dimorphism and our relatively large penises and testicles, among other things, betray the tendency to promiscuity in our past, in which males used their physical bulk to fight off rivals and ejaculated masses of semen to "drown out" the competitors. When we entered an agricultural mode of being in our recent past, more stable relationships developed so that everyone could be connected to a family, and thus their right to access land and resources could be calculated and inherited. According to Potts and Short, marriage "is the badge of a polygamous animal struggling to be monogamous".[50]

Mary Clark accepts their conclusion but was unimpressed by the reasoning they used. She points out that in humans, sexual dimorphism is remarkably small relative to other apes. On average, men are somewhat bigger than women but the difference is far smaller than it is in chimps and especially gorillas. She reports that male and female attitudes to sex and relationships are also very similar, despite popular media reports to the contrary.[51] Her work emphasises that, as Potts said above, human *animals*, not just human males, "struggle to be monogamous."

Clark agrees with Potts that "marriage" arose as small human communities needed to grapple with the concept of property and access to resources. She claims that in extant nomadic groups sexual relations are relatively uninhibited, and monogamy is often absent. The whole community, or at least several males, help raise each child.[52] At the very least, because of the different environments in which human communities live,

---

[49] Potts and Short, *Ever since Adam and Eve: The Evolution of Human Sexuality*, pp. 92, 211.
[50] Ibid., p. 82.
[51] Mary E. Clark, *In Search of Human Nature*, pp. 239-240.
[52] Ibid., pp. 241-243.

> *The creative solutions of many traditional societies to coping with sexual passion without disrupting social order put modern Western attempts to legally and morally fuse the two to shame, as distinctly unimaginative, not to mention, unrealistic.*[53]

Christopher Ryan and Cacilda Jetha popularise this view in their book, *Sex at Dawn*.[54] If you are one of the many people who have read it, you also need to read *Sex at Dusk*,[55] in which Lynn Saxon sets out to systematically rebut most of their claims. In many places her critique is devastating, in others less so. Everyone trying to describe the behaviour of our nomadic ancestors over hundreds of millennia is constrained by the lack of solid data. Saxon comes to pessimistic conclusions about human sexual freedom based on modern hunter-gatherers, but all of them suffer from relative resource scarcity, since they are surrounded and impacted on by agricultural or industrial societies. Her views may be truer in times of scarcity for our ancestors; Clark's may be truer in centuries or millennia of abundance, as small, isolated groups of humans endured climate driven cycles of feasts and famines. As Saxon herself argues,[56] human sexual relationships have adapted in response to their environment, usually in various forms of serial monogamy with hidden or at least somewhat discreet extra liaisons.[57] This adaptation of sexual practice to different environments is the important thing in terms of the main argument of this book. Our environments are very different from our ancestors, so we don't

---

53   Ibid., p. 244.
54   Ryan and Jetha, *Sex at Dawn: How We Mate, Why We Stray, and What It Means for Modern Relationships*.
55   Lynn Saxon, *Sex at Dusk: Lifting the Shiny Wrapping from Sex at Dawn*.
56   Ibid., pp. 35, 78, 81, 91, 160, 207, 214, 222-223, 233-235.
57   Ibid., pp. 5, 133, 171, 190, 203, 204, 331.

want to simply copy their sexual practices, but rather continue to adapt as they did.

That said, it is worth learning at least something about our past, and the instincts we may have inherited.[58] What can we infer about human sexuality before and after agriculture? We will then look at the Old and New Testaments as case studies of how sexual relationships adapt to changing environments. As with our nomadic ancestors, we are not looking to emulate our Old or even New Testament predecessors, but to continue their quest for an appropriate faithful sexuality, in our environments.

Pre-Agricultural sex

Ryan & Jetha view it like this. After a few billion years, sex and mutation resulted in the evolution of our species: *Homo sapiens*. Human men and women continued a common ape pattern of frequent sexual encounters, probably especially male/female, and female/female. After orgasm, the men needed a bit of a rest, so the women often went off to find another liaison, since they can orgasm multiple times, and sex is fun. Clark agrees with them that having multiple sex partners built communal bonds, enhanced protection of pregnant females, and fostered communal care of offspring. You don't just need to be well bonded to your partner, you need the *whole tribe* to look out for you. So pleasurable sex as a bonding agent was better spread around, rather than restricted to one individual. Early humans didn't really care which child was theirs, since they had no property to leave them anyway. In a frequently hostile environment, everyone's kids were more likely to

---

[58] I look more generally at the mismatch between our evolved instincts, inherited from our hunter-gatherer ancestors, and our modern environment in John, *Worshipping Evolution's God*.

survive if everyone shared the care.

This might sound counter to the idea of survival of the fittest, but in the short term, cooperative tribes were "fitter' than those who weren't, in the face of massive challenges like ice ages and occasional skirmishes with other tribes. So, we shared *everything*, and tribes who did that well were more likely to survive to be our ancestors.[59] Jealousy was either genuinely low-key, or socially repressed. Tribes where people didn't act jealously or selfishly were more likely to survive, and so our social bonding instincts came to override our jealousies, at least when resources were plentiful. Since humans didn't yet live in close contact with domestic animals, sexually transmitted diseases were far less of a problem.[60]

If they are right, these egalitarian communities sound more like the kind of communities Jesus called us to create, than the ones in which most of us currently live. Rejecting possessions,[61] not worrying about tomorrow,[62] and rejecting the centrality of the biological family unit.[63]

Saxon believes that sexual freedoms were more limited, especially in societies where women are dependent on men for

---

59 Clark, *In Search of Human Nature*, pp. 99-124.
60 "Two or three of the major STDs have come from animals," says Alonso Aguirre, a veterinarian and vice president for conservation medicine at Wildlife Trust. "We know, for example, that gonorrhoea came from cattle to humans. Syphilis also came to humans from cattle or sheep many centuries ago, possibly sexually." The most recent, as well as the deadliest, STD to migrate to humans is HIV, which hunters acquired from the blood of chimpanzees. (Lafsky, *How Often Do Animals Get STDs?*)
61 Matthew 6:19-24 is one of many passages. Technically, ancestral tribes did not reject possessions, they did not have them yet.
62 Ibid.
63 E.g. Luke 14:26, Mark 3:31-35.

meat.[64] She states that although inequality between the sexes varies a lot in hunter gatherer societies, men usually have a slight to significant advantage. She doesn't document the dynamics in societies where the advantage goes to women, for example those in which foraging is more important as a food source than hunting.[65] Even when men had more power, women still had discreet extra-marital sex, often to gain more meat. Some even had multiple husbands, or at least fathers for their children. For the Bari and Aché, children with two "fathers" had the best survival rates.[66] Having too much sex too openly reduced their children's survival rates. The selection pressure also acted on the Aché men, whose children were more likely to survive if they remained with the mother to help provide for them.[67] Saxon's examples of multi-partner monogamy, and social monogamy with somewhat clandestine extramarital sex is still far from the "free-love" scenario envisaged by Ryan and Jetha.

We are still stuck with the fact that Amazonian tribes are agriculturalists as well as hunters, and very significantly impacted by outside pressures, so they don't give us a direct impression of our more distant, purely nomadic ancestors, who lived in relative or total isolation from other groups for millennia.

In her argument, Saxon makes the important point that sex originally evolved not only to deal with parasitism, but more basically to pass genes from one generation to the next. Evolution doesn't care about making us happy or fulfilling our "true human potential". Evolution is only concerned with our gene's transmission to the next generation. So, Ryan's assumption that returning to our

---

64   Saxon, *Sex at Dusk: Lifting the Shiny Wrapping from Sex at Dawn*, p. 215.
65   Ibid., p. 216.
66   Ibid., pp. 120, 128.
67   Ibid., p. 161.

"natural" sexual state – whatever that was – will make us happier, is not necessarily true.

Because of the lack of direct data, Saxon's dismissal of periods of more fluid human sexual bonding, as envisaged by Clark and Ryan, cannot be proved. The indisputable existence of jealousy in our day suggests that human sexual freedom has been constrained at least sometimes, and probably at most times. But our degree of jealousy and envy about other things like food, for example, or income, or friendships, vary depending on how scarce we perceive them to be. Sexual jealousy may also have waxed and waned as well, perhaps in synch with the availability of food, and thus the dependence of women on men to provide for them whilst pregnant and nursing, along with the dependence of men on women to gather and process plants to feed their children.

Whatever happened in our past, we now find ourselves in a world where women and men are increasingly equal in their ability to provide for themselves, and where sex – being separated from reproduction and protected from disease – bears little risk to men or women. Since this is a very different environment from that experienced by most of our parents and grandparents in the industrial world, both Clark and Saxon's versions of our history imply that our sexual relationships not only are, but should, adapt in response.

Saxon claims that early humans were largely socially monogamous, that is, we formed pair bonds, maintained by both love and jealousy, whilst keeping our other sexual liaisons mostly secret. Serial monogamy was common, but life-long monogamy not unknown.[68] Clark, and especially Ryan and Jetha, argue instead that we were polyamorous ('loved many') and overwhelmingly generous with our bodies. Even if they are wrong, looking at

---

68   Ibid., pp. 5, 190, 324.

our closest ape cousins, there's a good chance that our pre-*Homo Sapiens* ancestors were promiscuous, and that we retain some of that instinct. All agree that we were not biologically monogamous. That is, we had sex with other people, whether we had a main partner or not. And we did it enough to leave clues in our biology. Even if our mates, both female and male, jealously guarded us at times, there are clues that for 99.5 percent of human existence, a lot of sexual competition happened *within* the woman's reproductive tract.

Let's look at our ape relatives, compared to us.

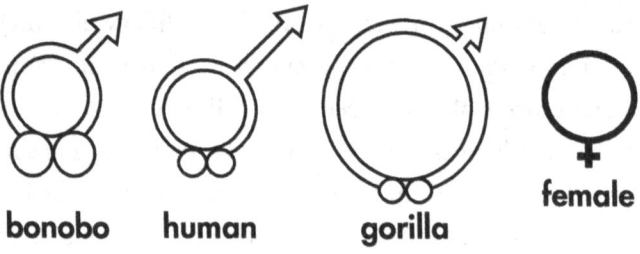

FIGURE 2 relative genital size[69]

Figure 2 shows the relative size of a male body, testicles and penis compared to a female, for bonobos, humans and gorillas. In gorillas, one gigantic male fights off competitors and so he has the women to himself. His is the only sperm with a chance to impregnate a female, so he needs little of it. He has tiny testicles, and not much of a penis for that matter. The competition to pass his genes on to the next generation happens almost exclusively before sex.

Gibbons (not shown here) are the only monogamous apes because they are scattered so thinly through the forest that they

---

[69] Based on a figure in Chris King, "Humanity's Evolutionary Heritage." The figure is redrawn from Alison Jolly, *Lucy's Legacy*, p. 180.

rarely encounter each other. Again, they have small testicles, because there are no other males around to try to do any inseminating. Competition happens before sex, in the process of choosing a mate, who then follows the male off into a remote corner of the forest. Recent studies suggest that even gibbons may be serially monogamous,[70] removing our last hope that lifelong monogamy is 'natural' for primates. In serial monogamy, males still only need tiny testicles because there is no competition to impregnate their *current* partner.

Contrast gorillas and gibbons with their big-balled cousins, the bonobo. Bonobos, a subspecies of chimpanzee, have *lots* of sex. Much of this sex is non-reproductive. Amongst the females, an agile tongue can greatly improve one's social standing. Saxon claims that bonobo sex is primarily joyless, existing to reduce social anxiety, and aid social climbing, and that much early observation of the 'sexy ape' was misguided.[71] Frans de Waal continues to insist that it is pleasurable and enhances group bonding.[72]

In any case, there is plenty of reproductive sex too, so bonobo males have huge testicles, to be always at the ready. This lets them mate often and gives a better chance of insemination each time as more sperm can be ejaculated.

What of humans? Our testicles are much bigger than those of gorillas and gibbons, suggesting that we are not naturally either polygamous or monogamous. They are not as big as bonobos,

---

70   Brian Switek, ""Monogamy" Is Much More Interesting Than It Sounds".
71   Saxon, *Sex at Dusk: Lifting the Shiny Wrapping from Sex at Dawn*, pp. 97ff.
72   For a summary of bonobo sexuality, see Zimmer, *Evolution : The Triumph of an Idea*, pp. 252-56. For an in depth look, see Frans de Waal and Frans Lanting, *Bonobo: The Forgotten Ape*. They explore bonobo sexuality especially from pp. 105ff.

but human men still make plenty of sperm, much more than needed for monogamy. It is also possible that human testicle size has diminished over the last 10,000 years since the advent of agriculture, as women's fertility became increasingly controlled (making us more like gibbons or gorillas). The diminishment may have been further accelerated by the increasing number of estrogen analogue chemicals to which men are exposed.

The suggestion that men have high libido won't raise any eyebrows. The claim that women also have high libido might. Until recently, and in many places still, women were portrayed as naturally coy, using sex primarily to keep their man happy, and therefore around. It was the price to pay for some cuddling. Common 'wisdom' as I grew up was that men wanted sex, and women wanted romance. The fact that this dichotomy didn't describe my own desires didn't shake my assumption that it was true. If woman have high libidos, but society assumes that they don't, what happens?

Since at least the fifth century, there have been reports of large numbers of 'hysterical' women who had to be stimulated by clitoral massage to relieve their symptoms.[73] Over a millennium later, in the sixteenth to the nineteenth centuries, doctors reported being frustrated by the large amount of time being wasted on such massage, though with three quarters of the female population 'affected,' it was a lucrative business.[74] Necessity being the mother of invention, this led to the creation of various mechanical contraptions and eventually to the home vibrator, one of the first electrical home appliances to emerge in the 1890s. Its effectiveness in stimulating one part of the body wasn't highlighted until the 1970s, possibly to preserve decorum, but also because of the

---

[73] From Rachel P Maines, *The Technology of Orgasm: "Hysteria," the Vibrator, and Women's Sexual Satisfaction*, location 365. (Kindle version)
[74] Ibid., location 160ff. (Kindle version)

feelings of inadequacy suffered by husbands in the face of a device that quickly and effectively produced such strong orgasms, in rapid succession.[75] For centuries, if not millennia, Western women weren't getting enough sex, and it had either driven them 'crazy' or into their local appliance store.

Until recent decades, an overwhelming Western assumption was that proper, normal sex is intercourse in the 'missionary position' and that the 70-90 per cent of women who don't orgasm in that situation were therefore abnormal, or frigid.[76] According to Freud and the many he influenced, childhood fixations were the issue, not an over-reliance on the missionary position.[77] I wonder how much lower my own libido might be if I never orgasmed during sex. Imagine a world where 90 per cent of men got to have sex but never orgasmed, and every woman orgasmed every time.

Doctors recognised the benefits of orgasm for women but restricted the appropriate experience of them to intercourse.[78] Any women who used their fingers or appliances to self-treat their 'hysteria' had to contend with a massive burden of guilt and shame driven by a concerted campaign to stigmatise masturbation, for both men and women. Kellogg's cornflakes were specifically designed to avoid stimulating the passions that might lead to masturbation. At the urging of Kellogg and others, baby boys were circumcised to reduce masturbation. Whilst clitoridectomies were saved for the most resistant cases,[79] girls still had various painful

---

75   Ibid., location 1229ff. (Kindle version)
76   Ibid., location 208. (Kindle version)
77   Ibid., location 645. (Kindle version)
78   Ibid., location 760-777. (Kindle version)
79   John Harvey Kellogg, *Ladies' Guide in Health and Disease: Girlhood, Maidenhood, Wifehood, Motherhood*, pp. 546-7.

powders applied to the clitoris to suppress desire.[80]

In a society where the missionary position is 'normal' and masturbation is prohibited, it's no wonder that most women gave up on sex and/or became 'hysterical'. Homosexuality, perhaps the only other avenue for relief, was illegal.

This multi-pronged repression of women's libido was so successful that Lord Acton, in 1875, was able to ignore the queues of women lining up for mechanical massage, and breathe a sigh of relief that, 'the majority of women, happily for them and for society, are not much troubled by sexual feeling of any kind'.[81] The need for women's libido to be constrained for a stable society was echoed by Richard von Krafft-Ebing, who claimed that, 'Woman, however, *when physically and mentally normal and properly educated*, has but little sensual desire. If it were otherwise, marriage and family life would be empty words'.[82]

Such normal and proper women are basically prostitutes, having sex not because they want to, but instead exchanging sexual favours for a share of their husband's fortune and to keep him around as provider whilst they nurture the children. This is the story which, even if true during hard times in hunter-gatherer societies, really gathered steam with agricultural societies, like the one created by the Jewish people upon their settling of the 'Promised Land'. Lifelong marriage became the norm (unless the man changed his mind) and women, bereft of all property rights, became totally dependent on, and indeed the property of, men.

---

80 For a summary of Kellogg's "contributions" see Christopher Ryan and Cacilda Jetha, *Sex at Dawn: How We Mate, Why We Stray, and What It Means for Modern Relationships*, pp. 285ff.
81 William Acton, *Functions and Disorders of the Reproductive Organs*, p. 144.
82 Maines, *The Technology of Orgasm: "Hysteria," the Vibrator, and Women's Sexual Satisfaction*, location 777-8.

Agricultural sex

In settled, patriarchal agricultural societies, consciously or unconsciously, a man is looking for youth, fertility, virginity, and *sexual* fidelity. In other words, someone to bear *his* children. Women desire husbands with wealth, status, good health and *relational* fidelity. In other words, someone to *look after* her and her children.

If the man and woman marry, from then on, his aim is to stop her committing *sexual* infidelity, so she can't get pregnant to another man, whilst trying to 'sow his seed' as widely as possible, to have more kids. She wants to stop his *emotional* infidelity, so she doesn't end up abandoned with the kids and, when she is ovulating, she is driven to seek out a 'real man' to get some kids with better genes.

For Clark, this is a radical shift from hunter-gathering. Egalitarian and generous sexual exchanges are undone by the invention of property and inheritance. For Saxon, it is an intensification of the dynamic that was already developing, from the serial monogamy in which men and women tried to control each other's fertility whilst they were together, to life-long monogamy, where men sought to guarantee that their offspring received not just food day to day, but eventually their property.

This is the environment in which Judaism developed. By the time the scriptures were written, Judaism was controlled by men, so we might expect that the laws they developed, and the mythology which supported them, would be shaped to help the men achieve their aims listed above, and thwart the women's aims. We would be correct.

Let's look first at the mythology that justified a system of laws enabling men to be promiscuous, while preventing women from the same. Here's Genesis 2:15 to 3:17 in a nutshell:

God makes man, then from the man makes a woman to be his helper. Recent attempts to make this sound egalitarian are noble, but in my estimation not convincing. The woman is beguiled into sinning by eating the fruit of the knowledge of good and evil, and then leads the man into the same sin. So, God puts men in charge of women, and makes childbirth painful for good measure. In other words, though it wasn't God's original intention, God's new rules for humanity are that men should control women, including their sexuality,

> *I will greatly increase your pangs in childbearing; in pain you shall bring forth children, yet your desire shall be for your husband, and he shall rule over you. (Genesis 3:16)*

To drive home the point about male authority, Adam's punishment begins, 'Because you have listened to the voice of your wife...' (Genesis 3:17). As we will see, this story also has far reaching implications for the Christian tradition, where 'Woman taught once and ruined all'.[83]

Let's look at the rest of the Old Testament. I will focus on the passages which might surprise us, and shake us up a bit, especially if we believe that our view of sex and marriage is somehow biblical. What does the Old Testament say about sex? What was the context? What does it imply about how we might live as sexual, relational beings in *our* context?

---

[83] John Chrysostom, 'Homily 9 on First Timothy'.

Sex in the Bible

Sex in the Old Testament

First, a positive expression of sexuality. In the Song of Solomon, we see a beautiful, poetic, erotic story. In Jesus' day, only married males over the age of 21 were allowed to read this. It's the Hebrew Scripture's sealed section, and it's the first bit of the Bible I ever read, thanks to my more churched friend, when I started scripture classes at school.

Some of our church forefathers, who themselves had very smutty pasts of which they were greatly ashamed at their conversion, and spent a lifetime condemning, struggled to see how this erotic book could be in the Bible. They tried to say it wasn't really about people but about God and the church. Which is hilarious when you actually read it. A small sample,

> 'You are stately as a palm tree, and your breasts are like its clusters. I say I will climb the palm tree and lay hold of its branches.' (Song 7:7)

> 'Your two breasts are like two fawns, twins of a gazelle, that feed among the lilies.' (Song 4:5)

> 'Awake, O north wind, and come, O south wind! Blow upon my 'garden' [nudge, nudge[84]] that its fragrance may be wafted abroad. Let my beloved come to his garden and eat its choicest fruits.' (Song 4:16)

---

84   'Garden' is a euphemism for a vulva

Unfortunately, the Song of Solomon is an island of positive sexuality in a vast ocean of sexist repression. Before we get to the worst of it, it's important to note that in the biblical narrative, polygamy appears explicitly in the seventh generation of humanity, with Lamech,

> *'Lamech took two wives; the name of the one was Adah, and the name of the other Zillah.' (Genesis 4:19)*

When Churches in Australia call on people to uphold the 'biblical norm' for sexuality, they don't have polygamy in mind. But the biblical norm for sexual relationships is *not* monogamy. Polygamy is a valid, and even commonplace occurrence, at least for those men who can afford it.

To skip ahead, even in the New Testament, polygamy was practised in Christian communities. Eventually, Paul starts to argue against it on practical grounds in his last letter to Timothy (1 Timothy 3:2). Here he argues that bishops and elders (and only them) should be the 'husband of one wife'. Much effort has gone into explaining why Paul doesn't mean what he clearly means, so you will usually see the claim that this is an argument against leaders being divorced and remarrying, helped by paraphrasing the Greek to read 'married only once' (NRSV) or 'faithful to his wife' (NIV).

Whilst polygamous unions have a strong Old Testament mandate, they weren't all harmonious,

> *'Sarai, Abram's wife, took Hagar the Egyptian, her slave-girl, and gave her to her husband Abram as a wife. He went in to Hagar, and she conceived; and when she saw that she had conceived, she looked with contempt on her mistress.' (Genesis 16:3b-4)*

> *'So, Jacob went in to Rachel also, and he loved Rachel more than Leah... when Rachel saw that she bore Jacob no children, she envied her sister.' (Genesis 29:30; 30:1)*

So, whilst polygamy might have done a reasonable job of attending to the welfare of women and children in a thoroughly patriarchal society like early Judaism, in which men were frequent casualties of war, women like Sarah and Rachel didn't seem too thrilled about it! Still, it was probably better than being abandoned in favour of a new wife, something which apparently happened often enough for the prophet Malachi to warn men against it (Malachi 2:13-14).

So, in the Old Testament, God says be fruitful and multiply, and that polygamy, for rich enough men, was a valid way of fulfilling that command. The other laws relating to sex and marriage function to maintain men's property rights while guaranteeing lines of inheritance. In this scheme, women are property, but they are offered a modicum of protection from being left destitute; not by being given independence and property, but by being found a new owner should their husband die (Deuteronomy 25:5-10), or by being allowed the harvest leftovers (Deuteronomy 24:19-21). That the prophets so often need to plead for the widow and orphan suggests that the system didn't work too well (e.g. Isaiah 1:17; Jeremiah 7:6; Ezekiel 22:7; Zechariah 7:10; Malachi 3:5).

We see this property approach to women and marriage in the Ten Commandments,

> *'You shall not covet your neighbour's house; you shall not covet your neighbour's wife, or male or female slave, or ox, or donkey, or anything that belongs to your neighbour.' (Exodus 20:17)*

Children were also property. If a male slave eventually earned his freedom from a Jewish owner, he had to leave his wife and kids behind,

> 'When you buy a male Hebrew slave, he shall serve six years, but in the seventh he shall go out a free person, without debt. [but] ... If his master gives him a wife and she bears him sons or daughters, the wife and her children shall be her master's and he shall go out alone.' (Exodus 21:2-4)

In passing, Churches rarely call on their members to uphold the biblical norms of slavery.

Even when love was involved, its path wasn't smooth, and women were still ultimately property. Consider Jacob, who loved Rachel but was *given* Leah as a trick,

> 'Then Laban said to Jacob ... "Tell me, what shall your wages be?"... Jacob loved Rachel; so he said, "I will serve you seven years for your younger daughter Rachel ..." [After seven years] Jacob said to Laban, "Give me my wife that I may go in to her, for my time is completed." So Laban ... made a feast. But in the evening, he took his daughter Leah and brought her to Jacob; and he went in to her ... When morning came, it was Leah! And Jacob said, "What is this you have done to me?"(Genesis 29:15-25)

And there was a lot of loveless pragmatism, including this version of match-making:

> 'So, the congregation sent twelve thousand soldiers there and commanded them, "Go, put the inhabitants of Jabesh-gilead to the sword, including the women and the little

> ones ... every male and every woman that has lain with a male you shall devote to destruction". And they found among the inhabitants of Jabesh-gilead four hundred young virgins who had never slept with a man ... and they gave them the women' (Judges 21:10-14).

In passing, Churches do not call on their members to uphold the biblical norms for warfare. Admittedly, the closing statement of Judges says that, 'In those days there was no king in Israel; all the people did what was right in their own eyes' (Judges 21:25), but the massacre and subsequent kidnapping of virgin farmers is clearly recorded as a faithful response to the need to keep their vows to the Lord.

The massacre also fits comfortably alongside those recorded in Deuteronomy 20, and the laws about rape and marriage. The rape of a woman was judged on property grounds. If she was engaged or married the rapist was killed, for he might be violating another man's line of inheritance. If she was a virgin then the Law preserved the social order, and her value, by forcing the rapist to buy her as a wife. It also provided her a modicum of protection – if you can trust a rapist not to kill off an unwanted wife,

> 'If a man meets a virgin who is not engaged, and seizes her and lies with her, and they are caught in the act, the man who lay with her shall give fifty shekels of silver to the young woman's father, and she shall become his wife. Because he violated her he shall not be permitted to divorce her as long as he lives.' (Deuteronomy 22:28)

Likewise, impoverished widows were granted a modicum of protection by the requirement for men to marry their widowed sisters-in-law, though even here the primary reason was to preserve their brothers' name. This is another aspect missing from current defences of 'biblical marriage':

> *'When brothers reside together, and one of them dies and has no son, the wife of the deceased shall not be married outside the family to a stranger. Her husband's brother shall go in to her, taking her in marriage, and performing the duty of a husband's brother to her, and the firstborn whom she bears shall succeed to the name of the deceased brother, so that his name may not be blotted out of Israel.'*
> *(Deuteronomy 25:5-6)*

If a man accused his new bride of not being a virgin, she and her parents would be expected to prove that she was. If they could not, she was to be stoned to death on her father's doorstep. If they were able to prove it, the husband was fined 100 shekels and not permitted to ever divorce her (Deuteronomy 22:13-21). Women are guilty unless proven innocent, and the crime of pre-marital sex is a capital one.

In the Law, men don't need to be virgins, but women might be harbouring someone else's child inside, undermining inheritance, and disgracing their father's reputation. So, women must be virgins at marriage, but it is assumed that men often won't be.

The use of prostitutes is simply mentioned in passing in the Old Testament, because it did not complicate property matters. Proverbs has this advice to young men,

> *'My child, keep your father's commandment, and do not forsake your mother's teaching… to preserve you from the wife of another, from the smooth tongue of the adulteress. Do not desire her beauty in your heart, and do not let her capture you with her eyelashes; for a prostitute's fee is only a loaf of bread, but the wife of another stalks a man's very life.' (Proverbs 6:20-26).*

Proverbs 29:3 does recommend against sleeping with prostitutes. Not because it is immoral, but because it squanders your money. For men, adultery is out, but prostitution is ok if you have money to burn. *Being* a prostitute, however, is a very different matter. Good Jewish men sleep with prostitutes, but good Jewish girls are burned alive for being prostitutes, if they are the daughters of a priest (Leviticus 21). Tamar's story is illustrative. Judah, her father-in-law, has refused to provide her another of his sons to replace her dead husband, and so,

> *'[Tamar] put off her widow's garments, put on a veil ... and sat down on the road to Timnah ... When Judah saw her, he thought her to be a prostitute, for she had covered her face. He went over to her at the roadside, and said, 'Come, let me come in to you.'*
>
> *She said, 'Only if you give me a pledge [of payment] ... Your signet and your cord, and the staff that is in your hand.' So he gave them to her, and went in to her ... Then she got up and went away ...*
>
> *About three months later Judah was told, 'Your daughter-in-law Tamar has played the whore; moreover, she is pregnant as a result of whoredom.' And Judah said, 'Bring her out, and let her be burned.'*
>
> *As she was being brought out, she sent word to her father-in-law, 'It was the owner of these who made me pregnant ...' Then Judah acknowledged them and said, 'She is more in the right than I, since I did not give her to my son Shelah.' And he did not lie with her again.' (Genesis 38:14-26)*

So, Judah thinks nothing of sleeping with a prostitute, nor of burning his daughter-in-law alive for being one.

Finally, we have Rahab the prostitute, who hides the two Jewish spies who have spent the night with her, and becomes a hero (Joshua 6), and even a hero of the faith in Hebrews 11:31 and James 2:25. Why was she a hero and not a harlot destined for the fire? She was a foreigner, and not the actual or potential property of a Jewish man.

The biblical norm for sexuality is that the use of prostitutes is fine, but that being either a prostitute or even just a non-virgin is death for women. Marriage to many women is ok. Raping a virgin is frowned upon, but punishment is simply to buy her and marry her. So, if you want to marry a woman who doesn't want you, just rape her before she gets engaged, and then she will be all yours. A marriage initiated by rape is ok, but one kind of marriage most certainly is not,

> 'We have broken faith with our God and have married foreign women from the peoples of the land, but even now there is hope for Israel in spite of this. So now let us make a covenant with our God to send away all these wives and their children ... [if any men refuse] all their property should be forfeited, and they themselves banned from the congregation of the exiles.' (Ezra 10:2-8)

When the Jews returned to Jerusalem after exile, some of the prophets, especially Ezra, were horrified to find that those who were left behind had married foreigners and polluted the holy Jewish race! Fortunately, the Old Testament is not completely given over to the xenophobic puritanism of the temple restoration period. We also have preserved the much earlier books of Ruth that feature a foreign hero who becomes the grandmother of King

David himself, and the book of Job, which emphasises God's love of foreigners.

That the Bible commands divorce in some circumstances, shocks many Christians, but not as much as discovering that it also commands abortion.[85] It really does. If a man becomes jealous of his wife and thinks she has had an affair, but cannot prove it,

> *'Then the priest shall make her take an oath, saying … "if you have gone astray while under your husband's authority, if you have defiled yourself and some man other than your husband has had intercourse with you… now may this water that brings the curse enter your bowels and make your womb discharge, and your uterus drop!" And the woman shall say, "Amen. Amen"*.. *(Numbers 5:19-22).*

So, to test whether another man has got her pregnant, the woman is given an abortifacient, 'the water that brings the curse,' and if she is pregnant her womb will discharge with a spontaneous abortion. The Bible condones, *in fact demands*, abortion in cases of suspected infidelity.

The killing of pregnant women, and thus their foetuses, is widespread in the Hebrew stories, starting with God killing every human on earth except Noah's family (Genesis 9), and continuing through to the conquest of the 'Promised Land', in which God demands the death of all indigenous men, women and children. To Judges 21 (above) we can add,

---

85   One third of Australian Christians say abortion is never permissible, and another half only in extreme circumstances. There are major differences by denomination: Pentecostals say never/extreme circumstances 50 and 40 per cent respectively, compared to 8 and 46 per cent in the Uniting Church (Nicole Hancock, Miriam Pepper, and Ruth Powell, *Attitudes to Abortion, NCLS Research Fact Sheet 14010.)*

> *'But as for the towns of these peoples that the Lord your God is giving you as an inheritance, you must not let anything that breathes remain alive.'* (Deuteronomy 20:16)

There is no 'biblical' argument against abortion, or murder, without a lot of selective quoting. To this we can add the scientific insight that approximately half of all pregnancies end in spontaneous abortion, mostly in the first trimester, and often before the mother realises she is pregnant. Those who argue that life begins at conception need to realise that half of all humans therefore die before birth, putting the decision to *deliberately* stop one more from developing in a very different context.[86]

So, to recap, the Old Testament sexual ethic:

Assumes polygamy, at least for the wealthy;

Condones having sex with prostitutes but not being one;

Recommends sex with prostitutes in preference to married women;

Insists on female virginity but assumes male promiscuity;

Makes men who rape virgins pay compensation to the father and marry the victim;

Allows men to divorce women except in a few circumstances;

---

86 Whilst capital E Evangelicals tend to take this position, they have not always (Matthew Miller, "How the Evangelical Church Awoke to the Abortion Issue: The Convergent Labors of Harold O. J. Brown, Francis Schaeffer, and C. Everett Koop"; R. Albert Mohler, *Roe V. Wade Anniversary: How Abortion Became an Evangelical Issue.*

> *At one period insists on divorce in the case of mixed marriage; and*
>
> *Insists on abortion in the case of suspected infidelity.*

This ethic evolved amongst a small but growing population moving from a nomadic to a settled agricultural lifestyle where men died in wars; men owned all property including women and children; unmarried women were vulnerable; non-virgins were killed, and barren women were shamed; where there was no protection from STDs, and contraception was limited to withdrawal, which was seen as sinful in at least some contexts (Genesis 38), and was probably largely ineffective anyway. In our day, one in five women relying on withdrawal get pregnant every year,[87] that's about *90 per cent* of women who use it for ten years.

The purpose of life and thus the Law was to grow the small population and expand the Jewish tribes/nation, maintain a stable patriarchal community, protect male property rights, and protect women from abject poverty.

Ellins asks what might have happened if the Jewish environment was different:

> *What if men were still being killed in war, but women also had control of property, and political power, and so didn't need the protection of a male head to survive… They might have revolutionised society so as to remove the fear and shame associated with singleness, barrenness, and lack of coupling. They might have discovered their identity in becoming chemists and physicists and invented the space age by the time of Jesus. Who can tell what creativity might have been let loose had women*

---

87 Anonymous, "Effectiveness of Family Planning Methods"

been free to think of alternative fruitfulness than sexual effectiveness and progeny?[88]

Instead, we ended up with a society which, to put it mildly, is somewhat at odds with what most people assume when they call on people to uphold the 'biblical norm' for sexuality. The point of this isn't to show the shortcomings of the Old Testament. The point is to show that retreating to a 'biblical norm' is no solution at all, since they lived in a different world and many of their ethical solutions quite rightly horrify us.

Some of this 'biblical norm' shifts when we find ourselves in the context of the New Testament, written some centuries later, in response to the life and teachings of Jesus, largely because their environment was quite different from that of the early Jews.

Sex in the New Testament

Jews still constituted a smallish population, now more urbanised. There was less war but more oppression under the entrenched occupation by the Romans. Men still owned all property in the Jewish system, but not in Gentile culture. In any case, Jesus was calling people to renounce their wealth, and in the early church people sold up their property. Husbandless Jewish women were still vulnerable, and barren women were shamed. There was still no protection from STDs, and contraception was no better. An initial conviction of the equality of women (1 Corinthians 7:3-4 [56AD]; Galatians 3:28 [55AD] soon faded (Colossians 3:18 [62-70AD]; 1 Peter 3 [75-90AD]; Ephesians 5:22ff [80-90AD]; 1 Timothy 2:12-15 [100AD]).[89]

---

88 J. Harold Ellins, *Sex in the Bible: A New Consideration*.
89 Dates are approximate and show a range of scholarly opinion, as summarised at https://en.wikipedia.org/wiki/Dating_the_Bible#Table_IV:_New_Testament

Very importantly, whereas earlier Jews believed that a Messiah would bring them everlasting occupation of the Holy Land, Christians came to believe that the Messiah, and specifically his return, would herald the end of the current world order. Jesus was about to come back and make all things new, instituting a new realm of righteousness, where previous claims to property and status would be irrelevant. The earliest, biblical, Christians believed that this new kingdom would be on Earth (Revelation 21); only later did Hellenistic influences refocus Christian hope on a disembodied, heavenly realm.

The purpose of life and therefore Christian teaching was to focus on the coming kingdom, which meant renouncing property and rejecting marriage as a pointless distraction. This paved the way for radical equality between men and women, since the agenda of patriarchy was now irrelevant.

In the New Testament, Jesus and then Paul apply the fundamental two laws of loving God, self and neighbour to the question of sex and relationships in their context. Take Paul's first letter to the Corinthians,

> *'It is well for a man not to touch a woman. But because of cases of sexual immorality, each man should have his own wife and each woman her own husband ...This I say by way of concession, not of command. I wish that all were as I myself am ...' (1 Corinthians 7:1-7)*

> *'But each has a particular gift from God, one having one kind and another a different kind. To the unmarried and the widows, I say that it is well for them to remain unmarried as I am. But if they are not practising self-control, they should marry. For it is better to marry than to be aflame with passion...'(1 Corinthians 7:7-9)*

> '... If his passions are strong, and so it has to be, let him marry as he wishes; it is no sin... he who marries his fiancée does well; and he who refrains from marriage will do better.' (1 Corinthians 7:36-38)

Why did Paul think that the unmarried would do better, despite being thoroughly Jewish? The environment in which he lived his faith was different from his ancestors:

> '... those who marry will experience distress in this life, and I would spare you that ... the appointed time has grown short; from now on, let even those who have wives be as though they had none ... and those who buy as though they had no possessions ... For the present form of this world is passing away.' (1 Corinthians 7:28-31)

> 'I want you to be free from anxieties. The unmarried man is anxious about the affairs of the Lord, how to please the Lord; but the married man is anxious about the affairs of the world, how to please his wife, and his interests are divided.' (1 Corinthians 7:32-34)

> 'And the unmarried woman and the virgin are anxious about the affairs of the Lord, so that they may be holy in body and spirit; but the married woman is anxious about the affairs of the world, how to please her husband.
>
> I say this for your own benefit, not to put any restraint upon you, but to promote good order and unhindered devotion to the Lord.' (1 Corinthians 7:34-35).

Note the equality of women and men here. *Both* are called to be disciples, focused on the affairs of the Lord.

Jesus expressed similar ambivalence about marriage:

> *'His disciples said to him, "If such is the case of a man with his wife, it is better not to marry"' But he said to them, "Not everyone can accept this teaching, but only those to whom it is given. For there are eunuchs who have been so from birth, and there are eunuchs who have been made eunuchs by others, and there are eunuchs who have made themselves eunuchs for the sake of the kingdom of heaven. Let anyone accept this who can..." (Matthew 19:10-12).*

If you can handle singlehood, avoid marriage. This is rare marriage advice. I've never met anyone who was given it, despite its clear Christian roots. It is misleading to say, as the Uniting Church marriage liturgy does, that Christ has blessed marriage. Jesus *was* against men divorcing women, primarily because it threw them into poverty, but nowhere does he recommend people getting married, indeed the exact opposite.

That 'Christian' political parties insist on upholding 'the family' and 'family values' is incongruous, in the face of Jesus' teachings,

> *Jesus said to them, "Truly I tell you, there is no one who has left house or wife or brothers or parents or children, for the sake of the kingdom of God, who will not get back very much more in this age, and in the age to come eternal life." (Luke 18:29-30).*

> *'Someone told Jesus, "Look, your mother and your brothers are standing outside, wanting to speak to you ... " pointing to his disciples, Jesus said, "Here are my mother and my brothers! For whoever does the will of my Father in heaven is my brother and sister and mother." (Matthew 12:47-50)*

> "Call no one your father on earth, for you have one Father – the one in heaven." (Matthew 23:9)

If gay marriage really is undermining family values, Jesus beat us to it by 2,000 years,

> "Whoever comes to me and does not hate father and mother, wife and children, brothers and sisters, yes, and even life itself, cannot be my disciple." (Luke 14:26)

Finally, to emphasise this new context in which possessions are not to be guarded and handed on to sons, but rather renounced,

> "Whoever does not carry the cross and follow me cannot be my disciple ... So therefore, none of you can become my disciple if you do not get rid of all your possessions." (Luke 14:27, 33)

> Jesus said to his disciples, "Therefore I tell you, do not worry about your life, what you will eat, or about your body, what you will wear. For life is more than food, and the body more than clothing. Consider the ravens ... Consider the lilies ... And do not keep striving for what you are to eat and what you are to drink, and do not keep worrying ... Instead, strive for God's kingdom, and these things will be given to you as well." (Luke 12:22ff; Matthew 6:25ff)

> 'Do not be afraid, little flock, for it is your Father's good pleasure to give you the kingdom. Sell your possessions, and give alms... For where your treasure is, there your heart will be also.' (Luke 12:32-34)

Jesus undermined capitalism before it even began![90]

So, we have Jesus demolishing the concept of the nuclear family, and even the biological family itself, in favour of those who do the will of God. He rejected wealth, and even the acquisition of possessions, because the time is short, and there is no point worrying about tomorrow – that will have enough worries of its own.

This doesn't sound much like the society or community in which I grew up. Or you, I guess. We haven't taken on the New Testament ethic of family, or possessions, or of resisting marriage. How on earth has the church ended up being the institution in charge of marriages, given our founder's teachings?

Well, because our environment has changed significantly since New Testament times. The expected imminent coming of Christ didn't eventuate and as it became the sanctioned religion of the Roman empire, the church became a tool for bringing unity and preserving the status quo, rather than upending it with visions of the kind of radical egalitarianism not known since our pre-agricultural days. Let's look at this shift from pre-human, to Old Testament, to New Testament relationships in another way, through the lens of the evolution of Jesus' two commandments.

Love your neighbour

In the context of the evolution of the love of God, self, and neighbour, love isn't a romantic feeling, but a commitment. Love is actions on behalf of the beloved.

---

90 Though as Paul Babie, a Ukranian Catholic priest in Adelaide, pointed out in a talk I attended years ago, not all of Jesus' followers gave away all their possessions, see Luke 8 for example.

Pre-human social species, from dogs to chimps to *Homo erectus*, had an approach we might call 'love yourself, and support your neighbour'. The neighbour is the pack or community, and often the partner(s) when there were young to be cared for. The goal of life was to maximise breeding and protect young, which involved guarding territory together.

Our hunter-gatherer ancestors probably continued this, though with a growing sense of the need to love the gods in recent millennia.[91] In the Old Testament, the neighbour was the tribe, perhaps the nation: the other Jews who kept the same Law. A goal of life was to maximise breeding and protect property, which involved men guarding territory together against enemies. Guarding territory was connected to the idea of building an earthly kingdom of God. Life also involved guarding possessions, including women (especially virgins) from each other.

In this context, polygamous marriage was good, breeding was good, men were in control, women were vulnerable, contraception was minimal, safe sex was non-existent, prostitution was morally indifferent (for men), and barrenness (for women) was shameful. This was the era of 'be fruitful and multiply' (Genesis 1:28).

In the early New Testament, Jesus redefined neighbour as including even the despised enemy (Matthew 5:43-45). Family was redefined non-biologically (Matthew 12:50), and possessions were an impediment to putting one's heart fully towards the Kingdom of God (Matthew 6:21, etc.). Hierarchy was rejected by the one who came to serve not be served (Matthew 20:28). Patriarchy was rejected, as Jesus' followers were to call no-one Father, but only God (Matthew 23:9). The acquisition of capital was rejected (Matthew 19:21-24). If family members interfered

---

91 For the evolution of humanity's belief in gods and God see John, "Biocentric Theology: Christianity Celebrating Humans as an Ephemeral Part of Life, Not the Centre of It," pp. 177ff.

with the Kingdom they were to be cast off (Matthew 10:37), but men were not to dump their wives simply to take up with another, because it would impoverish and/or shame their wife. The goal of life was to increase the Kingdom of God through evangelism, not procreation.

After his death, the early church was convinced that he would return very soon to herald the Kingdom (1 Corinthians 7:29; Philippians 4:5; 1 Peter 4:7; 1 John 2:18; Revelation 1:3, 3:11, 22:7, 22:10, 22:12, 22:20), so marriage, reproduction and possessions continued to be seen as an irrelevant impediment to the cause, as they are in many modern cults. The church wanted to distinguish itself from pagan religions including the temple sex cults.

In the later New Testament writings, the authors are adjusting to the fact that Jesus hadn't returned, so people were encouraged to share possessions, rather than forsake them entirely. To give to the poor instead of becoming poor. The attitude to breeding was more ambivalent. The church was being persecuted and needed to fit in, so codes around marriage and more patriarchal relations between men and women returned, though they remained in unresolved tension with Jesus' egalitarian vision (1 Corinthians 1:11-16; Ephesians 5:21-33).

So, we see that even within the Bible, the values regarding sexual relationships, property and children changed in different contexts, as have the rules and guidelines to enact those values. How much has changed? How different is our environment? As with expectations around the return of Jesus and the end of the world, it depends very much on the one with whom you speak. The church still has plenty of supposedly apocalyptic Christians, but few follow the advice of the early apocalyptic Christians like Paul, by refraining from marriage. Nor do they seem to follow Jesus' teachings about renouncing wealth and property. If belief is defined by words and creeds, they believe in the imminent second coming; if it is defined by actions, then not so much.

The way I see it, the year 2000 was our last hope to see Jesus descending from the clouds. To keep saying that it could happen 'any day now' is just embarrassing, and, worse, it gives an ongoing excuse to sit around being 'faithful', passively waiting for divine rescue, rather than helping fix the mess we're making of Earth.

In the West, many of us have a nuclear approach to families and live far from our place of birth. We are less connected to our communities than people in Jesus' day. And there are a lot more of us. The 50-100 million humans living when Genesis was compiled, and the 150-300 million humans who lived in Jesus' day, have increased exponentially[92] upon the Earth, to more than 7 billion today. That's forty times more people on the Earth now than in Jesus' day, and 80-160 times more people than when the divine mandate to fill the Earth was encoded in the Jewish Creation story. Creation groans under this weight of humanity, especially those of us in industrialised nations. The number one thing we can do, in terms of savings of carbon emissions, *by over an order of magnitude*, is have one less child. In Australia, having one less child is over *30 times* more effective than the next most useful activity: living car free, and 100 times more effective than going vegetarian.[93] If that child goes on to live an average Australian lifestyle, in terms of consumption, then having them undoes every other environmental initiative the parent undertakes, several times over. And I have two of them!

So, unlike the early Christians, we don't believe the world is ending, but like them we have good reasons to stop celebrating

---

92 Southwood, *The Story of Life*, p. 247.
93 Wynes Seth and A. Nicholas Kimberly, "The Climate Mitigation Gap: Education and Government Recommendations Miss the Most Effective Individual Actions".

every new human birth, especially in industrialised countries. We also face a gap between rich and poor, which constituted a major focus on Jesus' teachings, and our wealth gap is growing. In the last 10 years, the richest 1 per cent of humans have increased their share of the world wealth from 45.5 to 50.1 per cent.[94]

Also growing is the gap between puberty and marriage, and thus the scope for pre-marital sex, something that barely existed for the Jews and first Christians.

---

94 Anonymous, "Global Wealth Report 2017: Where Are We Ten Years after the Crisis?"

Sex Today

The premarital window

The New Testament doesn't need to deal with pre-marital sex. The legal age of marriage for a Jewish boy was thirteen and a half years; for girls it was a year younger, and they were often betrothed even earlier. They hit puberty at about fifteen. Imagine a world in which you are married *before* you hit puberty! By contrast, we have a huge gap between puberty, which happens now at about age twelve, and marriage, which is most common at thirty. That's eighteen years to twiddle our thumbs before marriage.

Admittedly, men in Jesus' day often married later, when they were ready to start a household, but they were allowed, and even advised in Proverbs, to satisfy their sexual urges with prostitutes in the meantime. Girls were married young to guarantee their virginity.

Once married, you didn't have to make a go of it for very long. If you lived to be ten, your life expectancy was about 47,[95] so men had – let's say – 25 years of marriage, during which they could visit prostitutes, and if they were rich enough add more wives, concubines and slaves. Having married at 30, barring tragedy, I can expect about fifty years of monogamy ahead of me, and it's unlikely I'll add any concubines!

If men were unhappy in their marriage, it was relatively easy to dispose of a wife, depending on which school of Judaism they followed. Girls had about 35 years of marriage, and no prospects for divorce. With a shorter life expectancy, lengthy periods of single life after divorce or widowhood were uncommon. With the

---

[95] Karen Cokayne, *Experiencing Old Age in Ancient Rome*, p. 3.

median age of divorce in our era being 45, most modern divorcees can expect a long period of sexual vitality ahead of them, as can those who are widowed young.

Our environment received another major shakeup with the arrival of reliable contraception for the first time in human history,[96] at least in many parts of the world, and the ability to prevent or treat most of the sexually transmitted diseases which we picked up from livestock in our brave new world of agriculture. Abortion is now more available and safer for more women. It is, therefore, increasingly possible to separate sex from procreation. If we want to limit our runaway global population growth, we no longer must be chaste to do so. One day, perhaps, churches will stop automatically celebrating every new birth as a gift from God, and start finding ways to explicitly celebrate healthy sexual relationships before and after marriage.[97]

Before we apply this to the new context within marriage, which is where most Christians eventually find themselves, let's visit the pink elephant in the room of just about every discussion any church has had about sex, perhaps because it is a welcome distraction for the majority from too much self-examination, and it means there is less time to talk about the dangers of greed and wealth.

Homosexuality

If you skipped 'straight' to this section, you are probably in good company. The church is obsessed with homosexual sex. So much

---

96 Chickens have been onto it for millions of years, ejecting sperm of sub-par roosters with a few cloacal contractions, Zimmer, *Evolution : The Triumph of an Idea*, p. 240.
97 I imagined what that debate could look like on the floor of a Synod in John, *Worshipping Evolution's God*, Assembly Accepts call for Reproductive Celibacy.

has been written about the sexual ethics of the small percentage of us who are gay or lesbian that I reversed the emphasis in this book. Here is a summary of some key points, drawing largely on William Loader, a scholar with extensive experience in the cultural setting of the New Testament and its implications for how we interpret it.[98] Loader makes the point that although many people have read passages like Romans 1 closely to look for interpretations that are less hostile to gay and lesbian people, the text itself and the Jewish context in which it is written suggests that this won't work.

We can discern from Philo, a Jew who wrote prolifically around this time, and from Paul's writings, that Jews, including Paul, didn't know about homosexuality as an orientation. They saw straight people who, especially when drunk or lustful, gave up their 'natural desires' and had sex with people of the same sex, especially men using other men. In the light of the evidence of recent decades that there is such a thing as homosexuality, the foundation of Paul and Philo's rejection of same sex relationships is undermined. Our ability to reach different conclusions from them is strengthened if we also do not share their patriarchal assumptions about inherent male superiority.[99] In the New Testament world, gay sex upsets the divine and natural order. As we saw in our Old Testament

---

[98] Taken from his talk, an evening session for lay people and local leaders exploring 'A First Century Perspective on Same-Gender Relations'. He has written extensively on the subject, see http://wwwstaff.murdoch.edu.au/~loader/home.html. The pdf *Same-Sex Relationships: A First Century Perspective* gives a very short summary, or you can read the 150 page summary of his five volume work in William Loader, *Making Sense of Sex: Attitudes Towards Sexuality in Early Jewish and Christian Literature*.

[99] This is a minor point for Loader, but I think it is a significant factor in our wider culture, which accepts that homosexuality exists, but remains deeply sexist.

readings, male and female weren't just gender categories, they were hierarchical categories. In 1 Corinthians 11:7, Paul claims that man is the image and glory of God, whereas woman is only the glory of man.[100] Women were weak and couldn't be trusted to teach or have authority over men (1 Timothy 2:11-12).[101]

In that world, to 'use' a man as a woman demeans the man so used. When a woman presumes to act like a man with another woman, she is breaking the natural order and rising above her station. Paul also thought that short hair for men and long hair for women was the natural order (1 Corinthians 11:14-15).

Of course, not all Christians do reject a patriarchal understanding of nature, nor do many in those societies once influenced by 'Christian values'. But I am a part of the Uniting Church largely because its ministers are required to accept the full equality of women in all aspects of the church's life, including ordained leadership. This makes evangelicals very uncomfortable, because they realise that the equality of women in leadership, despite biblical mandates for women to learn in submission and be silent in church, undermines their case against a 'biblical' opposition to homosexuality.[102]

If you believe that both men and women were created in the image of God, as most Christians now claim, and especially if you believe that homosexuality truly exists, as even most conservative

---

[100] Paul's argument rests of woman having been created from man, based on Genesis 2, a reversal of the evolution of gender in the scientific creation stories as outlined above.

[101] Also based on the misapprehension that male existed first, then female, though probably written by a later Pauline disciple.

[102] Walter Abetz and Katherine Abetz, *Swimming between the Flags: Reflections on the Basis of Union*, pp. 154ff. For more on the conundrum contained in their work, see Jason John, "Pilgrims Cannot Stay between the Flags".

evangelicals now do, then Paul's presuppositions in Romans 1 no longer convince.[103]

In any case, whilst men having sex with men, according to the Old Testament, makes God so cranky that they deserve to die, there are many more kinds of people on that list, whom we now gloss over. For example, at least a few times I would have been packed off to hell with these guys:

> *'If a man lies with a woman having her sickness [her period], he has laid bare her flow and she has laid bare her flow of blood; both of them shall be cut off from their people.'* (Leviticus 20:18, Ezekiel 18:6)

Ezekiel continues,

> *'A man who eats upon the mountains, defiles his neighbour's wife, oppresses the poor and needy, commits robbery, does not restore the pledge, lifts up his eyes to the idols, commits abomination,* takes advance or accrued interest; *shall he then live? He shall not. He has done all these abominable things; he shall surely die; his blood shall be upon himself.'* (Ezekiel 18:10-13)

So, before we condemn same sex relationships, we'd better make sure we've taken our money out of interest-earning bank accounts and super funds and stuffed it under our mattress. If 'God hates fags' as right-wing religious fundamentalist protesters occasionally proclaim when picketing funerals of gay people,[104] then God also hates adulterers (Leviticus 20:10, Ezekiel 18:6); men

---

103 I suspect that Jesus shared Paul's worldview, being ignorant of what we now recognise as homosexuality, but on balance I don't believe he says anything directly or even obliquely about same-sex encounters.
104 Kate Dailey, "Fred Phelps: How Westboro Pastor Spread 'God Hates Fags'"

who sleep with their menstruating wives (Leviticus 20:18, Ezekiel 18:6); bankers and investors (Ezekiel 18:8); and superannuation and investment account holders (Ezekiel 18:8). God also hates shellfish (Leviticus 11:10) and polyester (Leviticus 19:19), but then who doesn't?

William Loader offers three options for Christians trying to understand homosexuality: Option 1 is to embrace Paul's view that same-sex sex is sinful, akin to idolatry, because homosexuality doesn't really exist, and same-sex sex is straight people rejecting their natural, God-given desires. And secondarily, it messes with the divine sexual hierarchy. This is required of biblical fundamentalists and literalists. In this approach, straight people whose desires have in some way been broken, must not act on their unnatural desires, but seek healing or remain celibate. However, even many conservative Christians now acknowledge that the various 'therapies', which this view has led to, don't work and even cause terrible trauma. For example, the founder of the biggest conversion therapy system in the USA, *Exodus*, resigned and apologised to gay people for all the harm the organisation had caused.[105]

This has led many evangelicals to adopt a second approach: To accept that same-sex attraction exists and isn't itself a perversion. Homosexuality is a real thing. However, like Paul, they still condemn the act. The tension is that in accepting the genuineness of the attraction, but imposing celibacy, they are putting a bigger burden on gay people than they are willing to place on themselves. The church's history in imposing celibacy on a category of people, rather than simply acknowledging it as a gift that some possess, has not been a happy one. The idea that gay people automatically have the gift of celibacy is quickly undone by talking to gay people.

---

105 Lisa Ling, 'Exodus Head Alan Chambers' Full Apology to the LGBT Community'.

Finally, Loader says, if we reject Paul's worldview, we should be consistent and reject the implications of that view: Accepting that homosexuality is as real as heterosexuality, and no more a sign of sin than the latter, we should put the same expectations of sexual activity on gay people as we do straight people and focus on challenging *all* our members to apply Jesus' teachings to their relationships.

While I was writing this book, Australia's Prime Minister tried to avoid a party room meltdown by holding a non-binding, voluntary survey of our willingness for gay couples to be allowed to marry. In my local paper, a letter to the editor challenged clergy to speak up publicly on the issue. Although I was pretty sure I would be saying the opposite of what the writer hoped, I decided to answer the challenge, in a way which serves as a sufficient summary of my thoughts for this book,

> *Last week [name withheld] asked for the churches to rise to the challenge of speaking out on gay marriage. Judging by my Facebook feeds and campaign emails I've started receiving, some Christians are doing just that. The ACL [Australian Christian Lobby] is very well-organised and well-funded. I assume the 'Ok to Say No' campaign is significantly Christian, though their website is silent about their constituency, because it's started spamming my church email account.*
>
> *As a minister in the Uniting Church, here is my attempt to rise to the challenge of speaking out. I write as an individual leader in the church, not on behalf of the church, which continues to create spaces for grace, to discuss this issue together.*

I hope we can say yes to gay marriage, get on with it, then get back to the actual threats to our families and children, like climate change and the growing gap between rich and poor.

Saying 'no' is not defending traditional marriage. Marriage as we celebrate it today is not derived from biblical traditions, nor would we want it to be. It isn't even the same as 1970s Australia, as I'll show. The Bible shows a clear development in the role and understanding of marriage, so if we are to be 'biblical', we need to be open to continuing to reshape the role and form of marriage in our context.

Some examples. Starting with the Hebrew Scriptures, it was normal for marriages to be polygamous (Genesis 4:19 is the first example). This practice probably continued into Christian communities, where Paul calls on elders (and them only) to be the husband of only one wife (1 Timothy 3) – this almost certainly isn't about divorcees, but polygamists.

Concubines were also a common addition to the family, for rich men. More importantly, all Old Testament marriage laws are based on women being property: an asset transferred from the father to the husband. So, for example, if a man rapes a virgin who is not promised to another, he must marry her (Deuteronomy 22)! If a man died leaving his wife childless, his brother was forced to marry her (Deuteronomy 25). Proverbs 29 advises men to have sex with prostitutes rather than married women because it's safer, and cheap (Proverbs 29). The story of Tamar (Genesis 38) shows that for married men to use prostitutes was morally fine, but for women to be prostitutes was a death sentence. Ezra 10 shows us that, for a time at least, mixed marriages were outlawed. Those Jews who had married foreigners were forced to divorce them.

So traditional marriage, as described in the Old Testament, was an institution whereby the ownership of a woman transferred from her father to her husband, who could have as many wives as he could afford (and foreign concubines). Men could also supplement their sexual appetites with prostitutes, but not with other men's property. After the return from exile marriage was used to preserve racial purity. When Christians say they want to preserve traditional marriage, they seem to mean none of this.

Moving to the Christian Scriptures, we see that Jesus was deeply ambivalent about both the idea of biological family (Luke 14), and marriage (Matthew 19). Let those who can abstain from marriage do so. Paul was even clearer that it was better not to marry, though he conceded that it wasn't a sin (1 Corinthians). Why? Because Paul, and probably Jesus, believed that the world was going to end soon, and marriage was a distraction. Jesus also wanted people to be loyal to God, not the patriarch of their family. Jesus did also argue against divorce, but a close look at the texts and contexts suggests that this had more to do with protecting Jewish women from the financial devastation they suffered when their husbands dumped them. Churches which are arguing against gay marriage are not arguing against allowing people to remarry, despite Jesus' apparently clear teachings against it.

Paul, and probably Jesus, were against sex outside of marriage, for men and women. So, for millennia the church has emphasised that the only legitimate form of sexual relationship is a married one. Gay and lesbian people are therefore in a bind: they can't marry; therefore, they can never legitimately have sex in conservative Christianity. It is completely disingenuous to now say that de facto relationships are just as good as marriage, so gay couples don't need access to the latter. Of course, many/most of the churches arguing against gay marriage, whatever arguments they are raising publicly, are coming from a place of rejecting the legitimacy of any homosexual relationship whatsoever. Therefore, they can never accept gay marriage even if every objection they raise is adequately answered.

In later letters (Colossians, Ephesians, Hebrews), marriage is more esteemed, as a way of preserving stability and the church's good name in society, and in preserving the patriarchal structure the church had returned to, after the radical egalitarianism of Jesus and Paul. Christians who ignore Jesus and Paul's ambivalence and focus on the later writings when they talk about 'traditional marriage' are faced with the sexism at its core. Some, like the Sydney Anglicans, have no problem defending a sexist view of marriage: men are meant to be the head of the household, the ones with ultimate authority. Wives are to submit to them 'as to the Lord'. The husband is head of his wife as Christ is head of the church (Ephesians 5).

Perhaps the problem with gay marriage is that it won't be clear who has to do the submitting, and who gets to be the Lord.

This website, which is defending a biblical view of marriage, summarises the implications perfectly:

'God never meant for women to have to balance a career and family obligations as men are meant to do. A woman's complete focus was meant to be on serving the needs of her husband, her children and her home.' (biblicalgenderroles.com)

For a church to argue that they are defending traditional marriage, without accepting that we are therefore defending fundamentally sexist marriage, is hypocritical. Because of our Christian heritage, only since 1970 has 'traditional marriage' not meant that women were forced to resign from their careers to become good wives.

If we allow that marriage these days is rooted in a couples' free choice to marry for love, rather than being a property transaction, and that men and women should be equals in that relationship, then we are absolutely not defending biblical marriage, or even traditional Western marriage. If we allow that these developments (love and equality between sexes) are a good thing, then we are forced to be open to the idea that same sex marriage – now that gay and lesbian people have attained the rights that women gained in the '60s – is a legitimate development in this new context.

Some of us might still disagree with it, but there is no basis on which to play the 'biblical', 'Christian', or 'traditional' card. We have dropped many aspects of traditional marriage in the past, and good riddance to all of it.

We live in a very different world from Ezra, and Jesus and Paul. Marriage already looks very different from how they understood it. We live in a less sexist world than the '50s, and marriage has changed to reflect that. We live in a less homophobic world than the '80s, how should marriage reflect that?

The actual tradition of marriage is that it constantly changes to reflect our society's growing acceptance of difference. That is a tradition I'm happy to say yes to continuing.

Everything said about homosexuality applies to bisexuality. Although the existence of truly bisexual people has often been disputed by academics and activists, increasing evidence suggests that some people are attracted to both sexes.[106] From 2006 to 2008, the Centre for Disease Control and Prevention's *National Survey of Family Growth* surveyed Americans on their sexual orientation and found that 16 per cent of women and 5 per cent of men declined to select straight or gay, insisting that they were somewhere in the middle, attracted to both genders to varying degrees. In the NHIS survey (National Health Interview Survey [a US study]) in 2013, 1.6 per cent of adults identified as gay or lesbian, and 0.7

---

106 Michael Castelman, 'The Continuing Controversy Over Bisexuality'.

per cent identified as bisexual.[107] When scientists asked people's genitals directly, by sticking probes on them before showing their owners diverse types of pornography, women exhibited remarkably greater flexibility in what aroused them, even when they denied it in the accompanying questionnaire.[108] If they were answering honestly (and they don't, when asked about frequency of sexual encounters),[109] this suggests that social conditioning is able to repress not just women's willingness to admit to arousal, but even their conscious awareness of it.

Whatever our sexual orientation, we are joined by our common interest in one activity, even if through great force of will, and backed by massive societal pressure, we never participate:

Masturbation

> *'I just want to make love to myself – it's better for my sexual and mental health.'*[110]

At school, my best friend Adam had a dog with a very uninhibited relationship with her clitoris, and the flexibility to tend to that relationship frequently. Closer to home, evolutionarily speaking, I had the opportunity to observe vervet monkeys for a few hours in their natural habitat. If human men adopted the same nonchalance and enthusiasm for 'self pleasure' as our vervet cousins, one would

---

107 B. W. Ward et al, 'Sexual Orientation and Health Among U.S. Adults: National Health Interview Survey, 2013'.
108 Ryan and Jetha, *Sex at Dawn: How We Mate, Why We Stray, and What It Means for Modern Relationships*, pp. 272ff. M. L. Chivers et al., "A Sex Difference in the Specificity of Sexual Arousal."
109 Ryan and Jetha, *Sex at Dawn: How We Mate, Why We Stray, and What It Means for Modern Relationships*, pp. 277-278.
110 Isis, self-titled, 1994, https://isisbrisbane.bandcamp.com/releases

have to be extremely careful walking down the footpath.

Those two titbits were pretty much the sum of my knowledge about masturbation until I did some research for the talk on which this book is based. When growing up, I wasn't ever told that masturbation was bad. Or good. It wasn't talked about at all, so I guess like most things which are not talked about, I absorbed the idea that it was, somehow, kind of shameful, or at least embarrassing. The wet dreams I had certainly were.

'Self-pleasure' is, of course, a euphemism. Western Christendom preferred dysphemisms, starting with self-pollution, or self-abuse, which was claimed to cause everything from pimples to rheumatism, muddle-headedness, haemorrhoids, insanity and even death![111]

As mentioned earlier, Kellogg's cornflakes were formulated specifically to prevent 'self-abuse', and if that didn't work, Dr Kellogg was an enthusiastic advocate of circumcision, and in serious cases of sewing boy's penises into their foreskin, to stop masturbation. Girls' enthusiasm could be curbed by smearing the clitoris with carbolic acid, and if the disease continued into adulthood, by removing it altogether.

So, throw out your cornflakes, because scientists now tell us that masturbation has several psychological and biological benefits. If you don't have a raft of hang-ups about it, it can help stave off depression, and improve the immune system. Men who ejaculate at least 21 times a month were found to be 20 per cent less likely

---

111 Anonymous, *Onania: Or, the Heinous Sin of Self-Pollution and All Its Frightful Consequences (in Both Sexes) Considered with Spiritual and Physical Advice to Those Who Have Already Injured Themselves by This Abominable Practice*. Léopold Deslandes, Léopold Deslandes, *A Treatise on the Diseases Produced by Onanism, Masturbation, Self-Pollution, and Other Excesses*. Sylvester Graham, *A Lecture to Young Men on Chastity: Intended Also for the Serious Consideration of Parents and Guardians*.

to develop prostate cancer than those who ejaculated four to seven times a month.[112] So, if men find themselves single for any length of time, or having intercourse less than twenty times a month, they had better get cracking. By pathologising masturbation, the church and the medical profession it influenced killed an unknown number of men via prostate cancer and left more women than necessary suffering from cervical infections, urinary tract infections, and perhaps even type-2 diabetes.[113] Masturbation usually leads to orgasm, which strengthens the pelvic floor, reduces stress, pain and blood pressure, and increases self-esteem. Finally, you can't get sexually transmitted diseases from masturbation, unless you are very flexible.

How did masturbation, since it's so good for us, get such a bad rap? The church didn't help.

Masturbation *per se* isn't mentioned in the Old Testament, but the 'spilling of seed' is. If it's because of a wet dream, the man must wash everything and is unclean until evening (Leviticus 15:16ff). If he ejaculates on a woman, she is unclean too. Deuteronomy 23:10-12 requires the creation of a special 'wet dream corner' outside the camp to which the men must go until evening. You can imagine the jokes inside the fence.

Finally, there is poor Onan, who spills his seed deliberately to avoid impregnating his dead brother's wife. According to Old Testament law, he was obliged to get her pregnant so that she could have a son and continue his dead brother's name. God was cross enough to kill him (Genesis 38:9). In a tragic ignorance of context, especially in the medieval period, the Catholic Church equated his spilling of seed with masturbation, labelling it Onanism. From

---

112 J. R. Rider et al., "Ejaculation Frequency and Risk of Prostate Cancer: Updated Results with an Additional Decade of Follow-Up."
113 Spring Cooper and Anthony Santella, "Happy News! Masturbation Actually Has Health Benefits".

then on, masturbation was something that God got really cross about.[114]

The New Testament doesn't mention masturbation, but Paul's constant exhortations to battle against lust and the desires of the flesh doesn't help. He doesn't specifically include masturbation, but it sounds like he might if asked. Jesus' most obvious contribution is to say that for a man to look at a woman lustfully, is to commit adultery with her in his heart (Matthew 5:28). This presumably includes fantasising about women. Men who masturbate thinking about calm ocean sunsets, or their spouses, are off the hook but the rest of us might be in trouble. Women's lustful looking isn't addressed, but in my experience, when a partner 'looks lustfully', it is less confronting than them actually committing adultery by several orders of magnitude. And, of course, Jesus goes on to command us to pluck out our eyes rather than sin, which most of us put down to theatrical exaggeration. If we look at the weight of his teaching, wealth-love is a far graver matter than self-love.

Changing gender[115] equality, changing marriage advice?

Increasing numbers of women around the world, especially in the West, can support themselves financially, and contribute to society in ways other than child rearing and managing a household well.

---

114 A useful, disturbing, summary of Catholic teaching from the medieval period is at B. A. Robinson, "Diversity of Roman Catholic Beliefs About Masturbation".

115 In the first part of the book, I talk about male and female as being our sex. That's the scientific use. Now I start to use the word gender, which reflects the theory that our biological sex is influenced by our cultural heritage and upbringing to influence how we are treated and perceived, and see ourselves, based on our biological sex.

Sex Today | 87

The relational dynamic instituted by the agricultural revolution is crumbling, in some places at least.

So, in my environment, men are still advantaged by the system, but less so than in Moses' and Jesus' day, and even than they were in the 1970s, when my mother was forced to resign from nursing as soon as she married. We are slowly regaining the radical gender egalitarianism of Jesus and Paul, at least as it related to women and men, [116] though, ironically, this gain is resisted in many churches. The resistance is both structural, seen in the refusal to ordain women in most denominations, and even let them speak in some, and cultural, in what is taught about the relationship between men and women.

FIGURE 3 Marriage books

The book on the left of figure 3 is from the 1950s. The woman is faded into the background. The advice she gets? Encourage your husband to go out frequently with his men friends, though it means leaving you home alone. Keep yourself attractive, though not offensively so (!), in order that your husband may be proud to have everyone know you are his wife. Bolster your husband's ego, making him feel that he is the most successful man you ever met,

---

116 We are much slower to embrace Jesus' vision of an economically egalitarian world.

even if that means lying to him. We've moved on from that, I hope, but there are still plenty of Christian books, like the one in the middle, telling men that the way to keep their wives happy is to be *real* men. To take authority, to make all the decisions, and to make their wives learn in silence and full submission.

Though the main point of this book is to begin a conversation about sexual relationships outside of life-long monogamous marriages, I believe strongly that such marriages have a place. The Old Testament is rooted in an attitude to women which makes it little more than horse trading, or state sanctioned prostitution, and the New Testament saw it as largely irrelevant as the Son of Man was to return imminently, but we can still talk about how to live our marriages in our new environment when men and women are more equal, and aspire to go forward together as a team of equals, free of both the state sanctioned abuse of the past, and any hint of interpersonal abuse in the present- emotional, financial, physical or spiritual. I remain committed to life-long monogamy, now that I am married, though Toni and I celebrate the anniversary of the start of our romance more than we do our wedding anniversary. The wedding was a public commitment to continue something which was already well under way, for the rest of our lives. For one thing, our first child was with us for the wedding!

In understanding the end of my first marriage, and in staying married these last twenty years, I have found the third book in figure 3, above, as confronting as it is helpful. In *Passionate Marriage*,[117] David Schnarch separates marriage from its role in child raising, guarding property rights, and stabilising society. Instead, he focuses on the growth of the couple. Or more accurately, the two individuals. He is very blunt about how hard it is to be in a relationship with someone who knows you intimately over an

---

117 David Schnarch, *Passionate Marriage: Keeping Love and Intimacy Alive in Committed Relationships*.

extended period. It is confronting, it makes you vulnerable, and it makes you grow, with all the pain that growth involves.

Personal growth can happen in shorter term relationships too, but Schnarch argues for the unique contribution of lifelong partnerships, claiming that when people want to get out of a marriage (unless it's abusive) it's often because they want to deny truths about themselves, which only a long-term partner forces them to confront. He sees intimacy as about radical honesty, even in the face of negative reactions from our partners. Ironically, for true intimacy, both spouses must be able to stand independently. This, of course, requires egalitarian partnerships, where neither is financially, legally, or socially obligated to stay. If your partner is not free to leave you, they are not free to be your partner.

Schnarch's book is not religious, but he is talking about faithfulness. Being faithful to ourselves by having integrity, and faithful to our partners through being honest with them even when we know they will not like it. By committing to go through the crucibles together, to endure. If that sounds like hard work, it is, but he also talks a lot about the passion of marriage, hence the title! My book is focused on building the case for relationships other than marriages, but for those of us in them, who want to work out what a faithful, passionate marriage looks like in the twenty-first century, Schnarch is a great place to start. I am confident that bringing his work into conversation with your faith journey as explored in worship, Bible studies, prayer groups will yield much fruit.

In the ongoing spirit of opening up conversations, what we have learned about our past adaptations to different environments suggests, to me at least, that faithfulness – that is loyalty, devotion and trust – need not exclude other sexual relationships, whether casual or polyamorous as a valid discipleship option for some. Perhaps the biblical practice of polyamory, divorced from its patriarchal and even misogynistic context, has a place in the modern world. As Siegel discovered,

> *It is rarely the act of sex outside of a relationship that makes or breaks a couple's ability to survive... It is the meaning we attach to the act and the way we proceed with the information once it has been made known.*[118]

In countries in which lifelong monogamy *is* the socially accepted norm, anywhere from 20 to 75 per cent of the married population have sex with another person, without permission from their partner, depending on the study you read.[119] I am not condoning that – secrecy and faithfulness are mutually exclusive. But the figure does suggest that people are strongly inclined to seek other sexual partners, and perhaps instead of defining such desires as automatically sinful, we could instead help people explore the pros and cons of doing such in an honest, faithful way with their partner. That is, I suggest, better than pretending it does not happen, or implying that the marriage is somehow dysfunctional or inadequate if it does. Indeed, one subset of married couples who are open about extra-marital sex – the "swingers" – report high levels of marital satisfaction.[120]

Although Schnarch deals with lifelong monogamous marriages, everything he says would technically apply to lifelong relationships which by mutual consent included other sexual partners, or even committed polyamorous relationships. Most of his work also applies to long-term relationships. So, whilst he argues strongly for the benefits of lifelong monogamous coupling, and it's the path I've chosen, those benefits are probably also

---

118 Alyssa Siegel, "My Cheating Heart: What Causes Infidelity"
119 Fernandes, "The Swinging Paradigm: An Evaluation of the Marital and Sexual Satisfaction of Swingers," pp. 8-10.
120 Ibid., pp. 19, 37.

available to other lifelong, or even long-term relationships. Much of what he says could even apply to life-long friendships.

A quick recap

For Christians, the aim is not to apply the first Christians' teachings to our life, so much as to learn from the way they adapted the fundamentals of Jesus' Way to their lives, whether they did it well or not. Our task it to seek relationships in which we encourage, and are encouraged to love God, our selves, and our partners, as well as the neighbours around us. To strive to do for our partners what we would like them to do for us, and to seek partners who are willing to reciprocate. Now that our eyes are opened to the many ways in which women's libido has been repressed or constrained, when we come to a sexual ethic for the twenty-first century we ought to reflect on Jesus' challenge, 'in *everything*, do for others as you'd have them do for you.' (Matthew 7:12). Christian men, then, are obliged to make sure that women get to enjoy orgasms as often as we do, if they want to. Perhaps *more* often, given their capacity for multiple orgasms. If we get away from the idea that penetrative sex is the only item in our toolkit, this might seem like a less overwhelming task. Mutual orgasm is another fruit of the Spirit. There's a sermon in that I'm sure!

Now that we know that people in different environments will, appropriately, develop different sexual practices, we are challenged to take seriously Jesus' warnings against judgmentalism when it comes to how we each seek to apply his trinity of love (God, self, neighbour), as we walk his Way together. As we prepare to pull these threads together into a tapestry of modern sexual relationships, we might agree with the Old Testament writers, that sexual relationships should respect people's property rights, take account of the needs of any children which might be born, and that their ending ought not lead either participant into abject poverty.

But we would, I hope, reject many of the ways which that was safeguarded in the Old Testament context, with its patriarchal assumptions. For example, rapists should be punished regardless of the property value of the woman. They should certainly not be forced to marry virgin victims! Fathers cannot simply give their daughters to good employees or guests. Not being a virgin before marriage should not be a legal matter, and certainly not a capital crime. Women should not be able to compel their brother-in-law to marry them, nor to sire them. We need to apply a 'what's good for the goose' approach to prostitution. Is it a valid outlet for sexual pleasure for both women and men, or off limits to both? If the former, how do we ensure that the prostitutes profit from their labour, rather than the recent rash of wealthy corporate pimps? The Old Testament's contextual approach to abortion is appropriate, but only once the woman, not the jealous husband, is put at the centre of decision making.

Other parts of the tradition might be appropriate in certain contexts. We might remain open to polygamy and polygyny in certain environments, if all parties find it serves their needs.

In the New Testament, we could agree with Jesus and Paul that biological family should not separate us from the family of God or undermine their egalitarian vision of economic and gender equality. Our sexual relationships should enhance our ability to follow the commandments to love God, neighbour and self, whether that relationship lasts an hour or a lifetime. They should nurture us, not diminish us, and be Good News for us, our partners, and those around us who matter, especially any children who depend on us. To get into the nitty-gritty, sweaty end, we should ask whether we are willing to do for our sexual partner what we would want them to do for us. And whether that's true of them too.

Paul removed marriage from its preeminent place as the norm and ideal for human relationships. We could do the same, but not agree that there is no other outlet for sexual intimacy. We should be open to celebrating other forms of sexual relationships in the decades-long gap between puberty and marriage. We might eschew marriage altogether, pursuing reproductive celibacy rather than outright chastity. If we embrace marriage, we will need to decide how to deal with our ancestral evolutionary impulses: will we bring variety into our monogamy, and strengthen other platonic friendships, or will we, in an honest and negotiated way, find sexual variety with others to enhance our core life-long relationship? How will we decide what to do in the twenty-first century, as we practise the faithfulness, honesty, mutual love and accountability that is required for those who walk the Way of Jesus in any century?

Four paths diverge…

Four paths seem to open before us.

One is to try to emulate our ancestors, if they were the swinging, egalitarian, polyamorists that Ryan and Jetha describe.

More common today is a lifetime of serial biological monogamy, though for many that still ends up in marriage.

Others might try for a balance, exploring openly social monogamy – in various forms of 'open marriage.'

Fourthly, at the other end of the spectrum from Ryan and Jetha, is to understand our history, our drives and desires, to better understand how to be one of the 25-80% of couples who report being biologically monogamous for life.[121] More accurately, we want to be part of the subset of that fraction who has no abusive dynamic within their relationship, and the even smaller subset who is still passionate in their marriage and glad to be there!

As an aside, Saxon may be right that our ancestors were mostly social monogamists having clandestine liaisons, but that path isn't one which is open to people who want a faithful, passionate marriage characterised by integrity and trust.

For the first path, the polyamorous path, to work, we would have to emulate not just the free sex, but also the hypothesised egalitarianism and communalism of our ancestors – a life with barely any possessions and no property ownership. People have tried to create such communities in the past, with varying success, but all of them are confronted with the reality of being surrounded by a culture which is exactly the opposite. So, even if women are equal *within* an alternative community and might enjoy sex as equals, unless they live there forever, patriarchy will eventually catch up with them and their choices. So, polyamory might be a nice place to visit for lots of women, but for now, only the financially affluent with secure careers might want to live there. Men who want to encourage women to embrace polyamory will need to start by working for a world in which women and men live in similar environments in terms of their status, security, freedoms, risks, and opportunities.

Path two – serial monogamy – is already a widespread practice, and often a positive experience, driven partly by the now

---

[121] Depending on what study you read, 20-75% of people admit to having extra-marital sex, as summarised in Fernandes, "The Swinging Paradigm: An Evaluation of the Marital and Sexual Satisfaction of Swingers," pp. 8-10.

large gap between puberty and marriage, and made possible by the economic gains made by women, and contraception. Amongst my peers, it was seen as a kind of training ground for the 'real thing.' It is quite widely practised in the church but kept very quiet. It's also fairly common after marriage, or between marriages.

For most Australians, serial monogamy eventually leads to marriages. For a significant proportion of us, that marriage is socially monogamous, which is no surprise whether Ryan & Jetha, or Saxon are right about our past. If there is any chance of this being a faithful and healthy way to balance our past evolution with the idea of lifelong commitment, it needs to be clearly negotiated and honest.

What of those of us who want to stick with the fourth path, to live out our days biologically monogamous, as we commit to in our wedding vows?[122] What can our ancestral experiences teach us? If Ryan, Jetha and Clark are right, an important part of ancestral sex was the nurturing of communal bonds. So, in what other ways can we nurture relationships so that we don't feel the need to use sex to do it? If we want healthy marriages, we need healthy friendships and communities. This is a challenge for me as the business of parenthood begins to fade since, like many men, I've done an appalling job of maintaining my friendships over the last couple of decades, with men or women.

Saxon agrees that our ancestors, even if married, usually experienced sexual variety, through having various extra-marital partners or liaisons. If at least some of that variety was fuelled by sexual desire, not just the need to enhance reproductive success, then how do we meet a desire for variety within the one relationship, using our amazing brains and our nearly unlimited imagination? I'm not thinking so much of using a variety of positions, places, and

---

122 Whether our vows explicitly include a line such as 'to the exclusion of all others,' it is culturally presumed.

gadgets, though they may all help. I'm thinking more of Schnarch's challenge to be fully present to each other.[123] Then every time will be a bit different, because both people are always in different head spaces. We learn, and grow, and our experiences in the world change us, and so we're always slightly different people. If we let our partner see that we have changed, and embrace the changes in them instead of fearing them, then variety will always be with us. Our environment constantly changes over the years, so our sex life might too. Being with a life partner ought to mean having developed the humour and trust and confidence to try things and fail without it seeming like a failure. Of course, that's not easy – it can be very difficult to allow our lifelong partner to see who we really are and what we really want, because if they reject it, we're stuck with the embarrassment for a long time![124]

Then there's the times when our partner is away, or in the next room studying, or even lying next to us. What role does masturbation play in helping meet our ancestral desire for variety? How can we use masturbation not only to nurture our biological health, but also as a source of variety and exploration which nurtures the health of our relationships? Can we combine masturbation and fantasy to experience variety, or does that constitute 'adultery of the heart' for you?

Knowing that sexual relationships have always adapted to the changing environment in which creatures, including humans, find themselves, frees us from dysfunctional attempts to simply reapply the morality and practice of previous generations. Knowing that

---

123 Schnarch, *Passionate Marriage: Keeping Love and Intimacy Alive in Committed Relationships*, especially chapter 8.

124 We can also feed our need for variety non-sexually of course, in ways our ancestors never dreamed of. We are surrounded by novel possibilities for stimulation, alone, as a couple, and with friends: television, sport, books, board games, gardening – the list is nearly endless!

some of their choices were damaging and dysfunctional gives us even more courage to take up the challenge of discerning what faithful sexual relationships look like in our environment. The fact that we all live in slightly different environments invites us to encourage each other to do our own discerning, rather than persuade others to copy us. The fact that our environment changes through our lifetime, as we change, and those around us do too, encourages us to revisit our views from time to time, and saves us from having to defend them rigidly at any one point in our lives.

Sex for *You* Today

Each and every human being on this planet is a unique person. Since marriage is inevitably a relationship between two unique people, no one marriage is going to be exactly like any other. Yet we tend to wed with explicit visions of what a 'good' marriage ought to be like. Then we suffer enormously from trying to force the relationship to fit the stereotype and from the neurotic guilt and anger we experience when we fail to pull it off.[125]

Your environment

What are you going to do with all of this? I have no idea, because your environment is different from mine. Since your environment changes throughout life, your answers will probably change too. But hopefully the following questions will be a helpful leaping off point for your lifelong process of re-evaluation, and help you to:

- Work out what your faithful approach to sexual relationships is in your current context;
- Live it openly, rather than feeling obligated to pretend to conform to some traditional norm;
- Encourage others to enter the conversation and journey with you.

Following is a short list of questions – none of which has short answers – for you to consider and hopefully discuss with people you trust.

---

[125] Peck. M. Scott, *In Search of Stones*, quote sourced from https://www.goodreads.com/work/quotes/651250-in-search-of-stones.

Your adaptation

>Describe your environment; how is it similar and different to that of:
>>our subsistence ancestors
>>the people of the Old Testament
>>the people of the New Testament
>>your parents
>>your peers
>
>How will you love your partner(s) as you love yourself?
>How will you 'do for others as you would want them to do for you'?
>What do you want done for you?
>What does your partner want done for them?
>How will you find a partner who is also committed to equality?

>**If you are married:**
>Why did you get married?
>Why are you still married?
>Does faithfulness exclude extra-marital sex?
>Have you had extra-marital sex? Has your partner?
>Is your marriage equal? What does equality mean?
>Is your marriage free from abuse, and who can you talk to if it isn't?
>Is your marriage passionate? What does passion mean?

If you are not yet married:
Would you get married? Why?
What does the gap between puberty and marriage mean for you?

If you are no longer married:
How will you walk the Way whilst divorced or widowed?
What options for sexual relationships are open to you, or are you open to?

Is your community a place where you can explore these questions, and if not, how can you make it one?
How can you continue this discussion with peers, and with others who have more experience of the joys and pains of living as sexual beings?

All of which leads to, how will you live a life of faithful sexual discipleship in your current environment? I'd love to hear your answers, and maybe share them anonymously with others, through http://ecofaith.org/christian-sex-today/

A final poem

The original drafts of this book finished with a poem that tried to summarise some of the main thoughts, and bookended "Sex is Fun". You can read it in my poetry collection,[126] though some of it is challenged by Saxon's work. I decided to finish instead with another poem that returns to those opening paragraphs which encouraged you to engage in open conversation. It is also a segue into the introduction of my next far more personal book, *The Edge of Acceptability* (in preparation).

I met a woman on a sexual harassment committee
leading to a dilemma
I thought she looked really pretty,
but did I dare to tell her?
And by me she was quite smitten
But we had literally just written
about how inappropriate
It might be to ask people out on a date

More alarmingly, to me,
she was a singer you see.
in a lesbian feminist band
Now you understand
my hesitation.

And she knew I was a Christian
And a Christian a minister at that
not yet legally divorced.

---

126 Jason John, *I'm not a Racist but I've got a Racist Butt.*

But of course
Sometimes you have to grow up, and take a chance
So I asked my friend to ask her friend if she could ask
Her if she could tell her friend to tell my friend whether she'd like to dance.
She would not.
If you've seen me try you'd know why
But she did want a root.
So we got together,
and a few months later I finally let her

Then we started on a baby
Who we took to our wedding –
Which to some extent was our way of getting
Some old church fellas off our back.
You see they were emphatic
that our love, no matter how ecstatic
must be chaste.

My minister was right
When he said, "hide the light
Of your love under a bushel, keep it secret, keep it safe
This may be blessed by the Divine,
But even if it's a pearl, there are plenty of swine".
But even straight white blokes like me
Begin to feel ashamed
If they accept that their love is one which dare not speak its name.

So I dared to witness, not beg for forgiveness.
Which sounds brave now, but
I would have quit a dozen times in the years that followed
Except for every Christian who confronted me with my disgrace
There was another who found us a beacon of grace.
Who thought "If he's still a minister, maybe I still fit".

And all the while their secret stories
Of celebration,
Hidden beneath layers of shame and alienation
Came quietly, circuitously, into our conversation
All these sacred little stories, feeling so alone
Because nobody dares to tell them in church
For fear of that first stone.

Why am I telling you this?
I want you to share your story of celebration.
Help make Australia a more open minded nation.
Go on
Take a chance
Tell someone about when you asked
the wrong person
at the wrong time
in the wrong place
to dance.

References

Abetz, Walter, and Katherine Abetz. *Swimming between the Flags: Reflections on the Basis of Union*. Bendigo: Middle Earth Press (self published), 2002.

Acton, William. *Functions and Disorders of the Reproductive Organs*. Philadelphia Lindsay and Blakiston, 1867.

Anonymous. "Effectiveness of Family Planning Methods." Centres for Disease Control and Prevention, https://www.cdc.gov/reproductivehealth/unintendedpregnancy/pdf/contraceptive_methods_508.pdf.

———. "Global Wealth Report 2017: Where Are We Ten Years after the Crisis?" Credit Suisse Research Institute, https://www.credit-suisse.com/corporate/en/articles/news-and-expertise/global-wealth-report-2017-201711.html.

———. Onania: Or, the Heinous Sin of Self-Pollution and All Its Frightful Consequences (in Both Sexes) Considered with Spiritual and Physical Advice to Those Who Have Already Injured Themselves by This Abominable Practice. London: H. Cooke, 1756.

Aquinas, Thomas. *Summa Theologica*. c1270.

Australia, Uniting Church in. "Uniting Church in Australia Additional Marriage Liturgy." 2018.

Bellis, Mark A, Karen Hughes, Sara Hughes, and John R Ashton. "Measuring Paternal Discrepancy and Its Public Health Consequences." *Journal of Epidemiology and Community Health* 59, no. 9 (2005): 749-754.

Beukeboom, Leo, and Nicolas Perrin. *The Evolution of Sex Determination*. Oxford University Press, 2014.

Castelman, Michael, 'The Continuing Controversy Over Bisexuality'.

https://www.psychologytoday.com/au/blog/all-about-sex/201603/the-continuing-controvesry-over-bisexuality

Chivers, M. L., G. Rieger, E. Latty, and J. M. Bailey. "A Sex Difference in the Specificity of Sexual Arousal." [In eng]. *Psychol Sci* 15, no. 11 (Nov 2004): 736-44.

Chrysostom, John. "Homily 9 on First Timothy." c400AD.

Clark, Mary E. *In Search of Human Nature*. London ; New York: Routledge, 2002.

Cokayne, Karen. *Experiencing Old Age in Ancient Rome. Routledge.* London and New York: Routledge, 2003.

Cooper, Spring, and Anthony Santella. "Happy News! Masturbation Actually Has Health Benefits." The Conversation, https://theconversation.com/happy-news-masturbation-actually-has-health-benefits-16539.

Costello, John. *Love Sex and War: Changing Values, 1939-45*. London: William Collins, 1985.

Dailey, Kate. "Fred Phelps: How Westboro Pastor Spread 'God Hates Fags'." http://www.bbc.com/news/magazine-26582812.

de Waal, Frans, and Frans Lanting. *Bonobo: The Forgotten Ape*. University of California Press, 1997.

Deslandes, Léopold. A Treatise on the Diseases Produced by Onanism, Masturbation, Self-Pollution, and Other Excesses. Boston: Otis, Broaders, and Co., 1839.

Diamond, Jared M. "The Worst Mistake in the History of the Human Race." *Discover Magazine*, http://discovermagazine.com/1987/may/02-the-worst-mistake-in-the-history-of-the-human-race.

Ellins, J. Harold. *Sex in the Bible: A New Consideration*. Praeger, 2006.

Fernandes, Edward M. "The Swinging Paradigm: An Evaluation of the Marital and Sexual Satisfaction of Swingers." *Electronic Journal of Human Sexuality* 12 (2009).

Gammage, Bill. *The Biggest Estate on Earth: How Aborigines Made Australia*. Crows Nest, NSW: Allen and Unwin, 2011.

Graham, Sylvester. *A Lecture to Young Men on Chastity: Intended Also for the Serious Consideration of Parents and Guardians*. Boston: Light & Stearns, Crocker & Brewster, 1837.

Habel, Normal C. "Bible Study Session 2- Humanity Sunday." http://seasonofcreation.com/worship-resources/bible-studies-for-the-season-of-creation/bible-studies-humanity-sunday/.

Hancock, Nicole, Miriam Pepper, and Ruth Powell. "Attitudes to Abortion, NCLS Research Fact Sheet 14010." Adelaide: Mirrabooka Press, 2014.

———. "Attitudes to Sex before Marriage, NCLS Research Fact Sheet 14013." Adelaide: Mirrabooka Press, 2014.

Hiebert, Theodore. "The Human Vocation: Origins and Transformations in Christian Traditions.". In *Christianity and Ecology : Seeking the Well-Being of Earth and Humans*, edited by Dieter T. Hessel and Rosemary Radford Ruether, 135-154. Cambridge, Mass: Harvard Univ Pr, 2000.

John, Jason. "Biocentric Theology: Christianity Celebrating Humans as an Ephemeral Part of Life, Not the Centre of It." Flinders University, 2005.

———*I'm not a Racist, but I've got a Racist Butt*. https://ecofaith.org/im-not-a-racist-but-book/

———. "Pilgrims Cannot Stay between the Flags." *Uniting Church Studies* 9, no. 2 (August 2003): 62-68.

———. "Sex & Relationships: From the Origins of Life to the Life of the Twenty-First Century Church." The Tops Conference Centre, Stanwell Tops NSW: Address given at Yurora, 2017.

———. *Worshipping Evolution's God*. Adelaide: Amazon Publishing, 2008.

Jolly, Alison. *Lucy's Legacy*. Cambridge: Harvard University Press, 1999.

Judson, Olivia. *Dr Tatiana's Sex Advice to All Creation* (Kindle Version). London: Vintage Books.

Kellogg, John Harvey. *Ladies' Guide in Health and Disease: Girlhood, Maidenhood, Wifehood, Motherhood*. Des Moines, Iowa: W.D. Condit, 1886. //catalog.hathitrust.org/Record/100479135

http://hdl.handle.net/2027/hvd.hc2ffh.

King, Chris. "Humanity's Evolutionary Heritage." https://www.dhushara.com/paradoxhtm/homo.htm.

Lafsky, Melissa. "How Often Do Animals Get STDs?" *Discover*, 2008.

Lahn, Bruce, and David Page. "The Evolution of the Sex Chromosomes: Step by Step." news release, 1999, http://www.uchospitals.edu/news/1999/19991028-x-vs-y.html.

Larmuseau, Maarten, Matthijs, Koen and Wenseleers, Tom. 'Cuckolded Fathers Rare in Human Populations', in *Trends in Ecology & Evolution*, Vol 31, Issue 5, May 2016.

Ling, Lisa. "Exodus Head Alan Chambers' Full Apology to the LGBT Community." Oprah Winfrey Network (OWN), 2013.

Loader, William. *Making Sense of Sex: Attitudes Towards Sexuality in Early Jewish and Christian Literature.* Grand Rapids: Eerdmans, 2013.

Maines, Rachel P. *The Technology of Orgasm: "Hysteria," the Vibrator, and Women's Sexual Satisfaction.* Baltimore and London: The Johns Hopkins University Press, 1999. https://www.amazon.com/Technology-Orgasm-Hysteria-Vibrator-Satisfaction-ebook/dp/B0044BBKWS/.

Mayr, Ernst. *What Evolution Is.* paperback edition. First edition published in 2001 in the USA by BasicBooks ed. London: Phoenix, 2002. 2001.

McMillan, Stuart. "Retiring Address to the 15th Assembly of the Uniting Church in Australia." 2018.

Miller, Matthew. "How the Evangelical Church Awoke to the Abortion Issue: The Convergent Labors of Harold O. J. Brown, Francis Schaeffer, and C. Everett Koop." Alliance of Confessing Evangelicals, http://www.reformation21.org/articles/how-the-evangelical-church-awoke-to-the-abortion-issue-the-convergent-labors-of.php.

Mohler, R. Albert. Roe V. Wade Anniversary: How Abortion Became an Evangelical Issue. *OnFaith*, 2013.

Pascoe, Bruce. *Dark Emu Black Seeds: Agriculture or Accident?* Broome: Magabala Books Aboriginal Corporation, 2014.

Peck, M. Scott. *In Search of Stones.* Pocket Books, 1997.

Pepper, Miriam, Steve Bevis, Ruth Powell, and Nicole Hancock. "Public Issues and Priorities for Churches, NCLS Research Fact Sheet 13004." Adelaide: Mirrabooka Press, 2013.

Pepper, Miriam, Nicole Hancock, and Ruth Powell. "Church Attenders' Views About Evolution, NCLS Research Fact Sheet 14030." Adelaide: Mirrabooka Press, 2016.

Pittsburgh, University of. "Two from One: Evolution of Genders from Hermaphroditic Ancestors Mapped Out." *ScienceDaily*, www.sciencedaily.com/releases/2008/11/081120171328.htm

Potts, Malcolm, and Roger Short. *Ever since Adam and Eve: The Evolution of Human Sexuality.* Cambridge: Cambridge University Press, 1999.

Press, Cell. "Cuckolded Fathers Rare in Human Populations." ScienceDaily, https://www.sciencedaily.com/releases/2016/04/160405161120.htm.

Rider, J. R., K. M. Wilson, J. A. Sinnott, R. S. Kelly, L. A. Mucci, and E. L. Giovannucci. "Ejaculation Frequency and Risk of Prostate Cancer: Updated Results with an Additional Decade of Follow-Up." [In eng]. *Eur Urol* 70, no. 6 (Dec 2016): 974-982.

Robinson, B. A. . "Diversity of Roman Catholic Beliefs About Masturbation." *Religious Tolerance*, http://www.religioustolerance.org/masturba10a.htm.

Ryan, Christopher, and Cacilda Jetha. *Sex at Dawn: How We Mate, Why We Stray, and What It Means for Modern Relationships.* New York: Harper Collins, 2012.

Saxon, Lynn. *Sex at Dusk: Lifting the Shiny Wrapping from Sex at Dawn.* Kindle ed. Kindle: Self Published, 2012.

Schnarch, David. *Passionate Marriage: Keeping Love and Intimacy Alive in Committed Relationships.* Melbourne: Scribe Publications, 1997.

Seth, Wynes, and A. Nicholas Kimberly. "The Climate Mitigation Gap: Education and Government Recommendations Miss the Most Effective Individual Actions." *Environmental Research Letters* 12, no. 7 (2017): 074024.

Siegel, Alyssa. "My Cheating Heart: What Causes Infidelity." http://psychologytomorrowmagazine.com/popuartic-alyssa-siegel-my-cheating-heart/.

Southwood, Richard. *The Story of Life.* Oxford University Press, 2003.

Switek, Brian. ""Monogamy" Is Much More Interesting Than It Sounds." Scienceblogs, http://scienceblogs.com/laelaps/2007/11/09/monogamy-is-much-more-interest/.

Various. "Bacterial Conjugation." Wikipedia, https://en.wikipedia.org/wiki/Bacterial_conjugation.

———. "Evolution of Sexual Reproduction." Wikipedia, https://en.wikipedia.org/wiki/Evolution_of_sexual_reproduction#Origin_of_sexual_reproduction.

———. "Sex-Determination System." Wikipedia, https://en.wikipedia.org/wiki/Sex-determination_system.

———. "ZW Sex-Determination System." Wikipedia, https://en.wikipedia.org/wiki/ZW_sex-determination_system.

Veyrunes, F., P. D. Waters, P. Miethke, W. Rens, D. McMillan, A. E. Alsop, F. Grutzner, et al. "Bird-Like Sex Chromosomes of Platypus Imply Recent Origin of Mammal Sex Chromosomes." [In eng]. *Genome Res* 18, no. 6 (Jun 2008): 965-73.

Ward, B. W. et al. 'Sexual Orientation and Health Among U.S. Adults: National Health Interview Survey, 2013'. https://wwwcdc.gov/nchs/data/nhsr/nhsr077.pdf

Warren, Wesley C., LaDeana W. Hillier, Jennifer A. Marshall Graves, Ewan Birney, Chris P. Ponting, Frank Grützner, Katherine Belov, et al. "Genome Analysis of the Platypus Reveals Unique Signatures of Evolution." *Nature* 453, no. 7192 (2008): 175-183.

Zimmer, Carl. *Evolution : The Triumph of an Idea*. New York: Harper Collins, 2001.

www.ingramcontent.com/pod-product-compliance
Lightning Source LLC
Chambersburg PA
CBHW010707020526
44107CB00082B/2704